The Wheel of Great Compassion

The Wheel of Great Compassion

The Practice of the Prayer Wheel in Tibetan Buddhism

Edited and introduced by
Lorne Ladner

with translations by
Lama Thubten Zopa Rinpoche
Lori Cayton & Khamlung Tulku
Dan Martin
Wilson Hurley & Yeshe Kedrup

Foreword by
Lama Thubten Zopa Rinpoche

WISDOM PUBLICATIONS • BOSTON

Wisdom Publications
199 Elm Street
Somerville MA 02144 USA

Library of Congress Cataloging-in-Publication Data

The wheel of great compassion : the practice of the prayer wheel in Tibetan Buddhism / edited and introduced by Lorne Ladner ; with translations by Lama Thubten Zopa Rinpoche ... [et al.]; foreword by Lama Thubten Zopa Rinpoche.
    p.   cm.
   Includes bibliographical references and index.
   ISBN 0-86171-174-2
  1. Prayer wheels. 2. Spiritual life—Buddhism.
  I. Ladner, Lorne. II. Thubten Zopa, Rinpoche, 1946–
  BQ5075.P73 W44 2000
  294.3'437—dc21 00-043822

06 05 04 03 02 01
6   5   4   3   2

Cover design by Gopa & the Bear
Interior by Gopa Design
Cover photos by Nicholas Dawson, Paul Liebhardt, and Venerable Roger Kunsang

Wisdom Publications' books are printed on acid-free paper and meet the guidelines for permanence and durability of the Production Guidelines for Book Longevity of the Council on Library Resources.

Printed in Canada.

Contents

Foreword

by Lama Thubten Zopa Rinpoche

ॐI'm very happy that Lorne Ladner has brought together here the incredible benefits of the practice of the prayer wheel from the various texts—the benefits of making the prayer wheel and of practicing turning the prayer wheel. Even Tibetan texts on this subject are not easy to find. I myself had to wait to find a text on this practice.

I heard about the benefits of this practice from Geshe Lama Konchog, who spent his life in Milarepa's caves and in hermitages doing many years of retreat, practicing guru devotion and the *Three Principles of the Path*, and doing two thousand *Nyung-nays* (retreats on the Compassion Buddha involving fasting and prostrations). He inspired me about the prayer wheel, explaining that the practice of the prayer wheel has unbelievable benefits. So, I waited for many years to find texts and asked a few lamas about this. Finally, Geshe Lama Konchog told me that another lama named Kechok Rinpoche had one short text that summarized the benefits. As Kechok Rinpoche was living in Australia, I kept it in my mind very strongly that as soon as I got to Australia I would immediately call him and get the text. So, I did that. Normally I am very lazy about reading Dharma texts, but this one I read immediately. The benefits described were a big surprise and caused much faith to arise. So, I put the text on my crown and then prayed to spread this teaching everywhere, in all directions. I made this commitment in the presence of the Compassion Buddha. After that, I built prayer wheels in the East and West, small and big ones, as well as hand-held.

In 1991, my students Lorne and Theresa came to Nepal, and I told them some benefits of this practice for purifying the mind and accumulating merit.

They then got a small prayer wheel from the market at Boudha Stupa. They became inspired and started to produce many home prayer wheels with microfilm and paper mantras inside. They gave me one, and I offered it to the king of Nepal. The Nepalese king asked me whether he should keep it. I said "Yes, and if you have this prayer wheel next to you at the time of death, then your consciousness will be reborn in a pure land of Buddha." Because he's Hindu, bringing up this subject was a little unusual. I hope he still has it.

Lorne and Theresa also offered a prayer wheel to His Holiness the Dalai Lama. So I want to thank them very much for all those prayer wheels they made and gave to many people. Now they're making available in English a collection on the benefits of this practice.

The prayer wheel is a manifestation of the Compassion Buddha's holy speech. Through this practice, one then achieves the holy mind, holy body, and all the qualities of the Compassion Buddha. Some readers may find some of the quotations about these benefits difficult. For example, in the text by the Fourth Panchen Lama, I translated a section in which Amitabha Buddha says, "Anyone who recites the six syllables while turning the Dharma wheel at the same time is equal in fortune to the Thousand Buddhas," and in which Shakyamuni Buddha says that turning the prayer wheel once is better than having done one, seven, or nine years of retreat. The prayer wheel is such a powerful merit field; by doing this practice, one accumulates extensive merit and purifies obstacles. The intent of these quotations is to give some idea of or expression to the fortune of anyone who who has the opportunity to engage in this practice. Turning the prayer wheel once is more meaningful than doing many years of retreat without the altruistic mind of enlightenment [Skt. *bodhichitta*] and without clear generation of the deity, lacking stable concentration, and so forth. It does not mean that by turning the prayer wheel once one equals an *arya* bodhisattva in equipoise meditation. I do think, though, that especially if one turns the prayer wheel with bodhichitta motivation while doing the mantra recitation, one will collect much more extensive merit to quickly achieve enlightenment than an arhat who abides for many years in the blissful state of peace for oneself alone.

Here also we can understand the quotation from Padmasambhava, in which he says that "even those lacking perseverance in their practice, who pass the time passively, will be able to attain mystic powers [Sanskrit: *siddhis*]. Those with perseverance for reciting the mantra and turning the wheel will undoubtedly attain the tenth ground [Skt. *bhumi*]; it instantly eliminates all the immeasurable negative karmic obscurations. Whatever mind-bound deity [Tib. *yidam*] you wish to practice will be achieved simultaneously. Even if one has no thought to benefit oneself, encouraging another to write the mantra and turn the wheel eliminates one's own negativity and completes one's good qualities." So, one can understand that this practice of turning the prayer wheel is a result of the unbearable compassion of all the buddhas for us sentient beings—whose minds are so obscured and filled with disturbing thoughts, like an ocean covering a whole city, and who are extremely lazy and ignorant—to guide us to enlightenment as quickly as possible. It helps us to complete the accumulation of extensive merit and purify obscurations so as to achieve enlightenment as quickly as possible.

When reading of the benefits, it may also be helpful to reflect that many human beings do not have the opportunity, the karma, even to see a holy object, such as a statue of Buddha, in their whole life. As just seeing such holy objects purifies the mind and plants seeds in the mind to achieve enlightenment or liberation, this means they don't have this opportunity to purify in such an easy way. In this world, the number of Buddhists is small compared to those practicing other religions. And even being a Buddhist doesn't mean that one is a Mahayanist. So Mahayanists are few in number, and even many Mahayanists don't get the opportunity to meet with and develop faith in this practice of turning a prayer wheel and reciting *Om mani padme hum.*

So those who get this precious opportunity are very few. This means you need to have a lot of merit, to be a very fortunate person, in order to have the opportunity to engage in this practice and have faith in its benefits. Even to hear the word "bodhichitta," one has to have the merit, so to be able to hear the teachings and practice, one has to have extensive merit. Why? Because this practice is the easiest way to purify all the negative karmas. Even the heaviest ones, the uninterrupted negative karmas, get purified through turning a prayer wheel. Even a fully ordained person who has broken all four root vows will get purified. Negative karmas are completely purified, one collects merit like the sky, and one especially develops compassion. It's the same as reciting the mantra—the particular benefit is that one develops compassion. So it's very good if, while reciting the mantra *Om mani padme hum,* you can also turn a prayer wheel. While you are doing your daily commitment or practice, reciting *malas* [rosaries] of *Om mani padme hum,* holding your mala in one hand, you can turn the prayer wheel with your other hand. Even a sick person lying down to sleep can turn the prayer wheel by pulling it with a string, as the Tibetans do in their homes.

Years ago in Dharamsala, I was very surprised to see Geshe Rabten Rinpoche, a holy scholar and great yogi who was my philosophy teacher, with a prayer wheel the size of a forearm's length wrapped in white cloth which he was turning by pulling a string. I was surprised to see this because it is not common for geshes in Sera, Ganden, or Drepung Monasteries to turn prayer wheels. I think that he was doing this because he was inspired by His Holiness Trijang Rinpoche, his root guru, who is also my root guru. His Holiness Trijang Rinpoche had built a prayer wheel in Marogang so that all the people there, old and young, could turn it as they passed along the road. It was built and dedicated for the purification and good rebirth of one of his attendants who'd taken care of him as a child and had passed away. So I guess that this unusual occurrence, Geshe Rabten Rinpoche turning the prayer wheel, happened because he was inspired by this root guru, His Holiness Trijang Rinpoche.

Regarding the practice, it is very good while you are turning the prayer wheel every day to recite a set number of malas of the mantra *Om mani padme hum.* It would be good to recite ten malas—a thousand mantras—for each realm: hell beings, hungry ghosts, animals, human beings, *asuras* [jealous gods], gods, as well as for the intermediate beings and even for the arhats and bodhisattvas who are still not fully enlightened. Six thousand mantras for each realm is very good; if this isn't possible, then try to do a thousand for each realm. If that's not possible, at least recite a total of a thousand mantras each day while turning the prayer wheel.

At the beginning, you generate the motivation of bodhichitta. When you turn the prayer wheel, recall:

> The purpose of my life is not just to offer happiness for myself and to solve all of my own problems; it is to free the numberless other sentient beings. The purpose of my life is to be useful and beneficial for other sentient beings—that is, to free other sentient beings who are numberless. I will free each of them from all their sufferings and lead them to happiness in this life, happiness in future lives, perfect rebirths, the ultimate happiness of liberation from samsara, then the peerless happiness of full enlightenment.

When you think of freeing sentient beings, you must remember all the sufferings in the minds of the hell beings, hungry ghosts, animals, human beings, asuras, and gods, all the sufferings that are explained in the teachings. Therefore, you resolve to achieve full enlightenment and actualize bodhichitta, which is the door of the Mahayana path to enlightenment. What makes it possible for you to have bodhichitta is having the root: great compassion. So, as you begin to recite the mantra and turn the prayer wheel, you resolve that you're doing so to actualize this for every hell being, every hungry ghost, every animal, every human being, every asura, every god, and every intermediate-state being. You dedicate everything, every turn of the prayer wheel and every recitation of the mantra, in this way.

Now, to give a general idea regarding the visualizations, if you recite ten malas, begin by purifying yourself. Visualize light beams being emitted from the prayer wheel. One can think of the six individual colors related to the mantra *Om mani padme hum* or even just of white light. This light comes from the mantras, and it completely destroys all the negative karmas and obscurations collected from beginningless rebirths. All of these are completely absorbed into the prayer wheel in the form of darkness and destroyed. Repeat this visualization a number of times. Then do this for all other sentient beings as well. One can do this focusing on all other sentient beings simultaneously or one can focus on the individual realms, reciting a certain number of mantras for the hell beings, and then going on to the hungry ghosts, animals, and so forth. Either way, one visualizes all the obscurations, negative karmas, disturbing thoughts, diseases, and spirit harms—every suffering—being absorbed into the prayer wheel. Then, after this absorption, light is again emitted from the prayer wheel, which immediately purifies all beings—wherever they are, each being's mental continuum is completely purified right there. All of their bodies become completely illuminated. At the end, each being's body becomes *nirmanakaya* in the nature of light, and each being's mind, completely purified, becomes *dharmakaya;* they all become the fully enlightened Compassion Buddha.

While reciting mantras and turning the prayer wheel, one can also meditate on *lamrim*—the stages of the path—especially focusing on the techniques for generating bodhichitta. One can meditate on the seven instructions of cause and effect for generating bodhichitta or on the method of equalizing and exchanging self for others to generate bodhichitta. This makes one's life very rich.

The prayer wheel can definitely be used for healing illnesses such as cancer and so forth. For this purpose, the practice should be done for at least one hour every day, or for a few hours along with meditation if possible. This brings extremely powerful healing. Even if the disease or the pain isn't eliminated immediately, this definitely purifies the underlying cause of samsaric suffering in the mind—the negative imprints. Remember that the disease is not the only suffering in samsara; it is just one small part of samsara. In the oceans of suffering in samsara, this is just one small part. So purifying the causes of suffering in the mind in this way means purifying the causes of all the sufferings of samsara. Healing this life's sicknesses is just one tiny atom among the reasons for doing this practice, which are limitless like the sky. Not only do we heal the sickness; we also receive help in stopping all sufferings, in having quick realizations of the path, and in achieving enlightenment quickly.

Now I would like to say a little about the essential benefits of this mantra, *Om mani padme hum*. If you recite ten malas—a thousand mantras—a day, then when you go to wash in a river or at the beach, all the water becomes blessed. Because your body is blessed by the mantra, all the water becomes blessed as it touches your body, and so the water purifies all the animals who live in the water, those who drink the water, and those who touch the water. It's the same as the benefits of the prayer wheel itself. All the animals who live in that water get purified and are liberated from the lower realms. Even those who drink that water will be liberated. Also, if you recite ten malas a day, then when you give a massage or touch others or they touch you, it purifies them. This is a great gift, much more special and important than being an ordinary healer, because it purifies the mind of karma and delusions and thus produces long-term benefits for those beings' future lives, freeing them from experiencing sufferings and making all their future lives lighter, happier, and more peaceful. By purifying their minds, it also makes it easier for them to achieve enlightenment. Furthermore, if you recite a thousand *Om mani padme hums* every day, then your children and grandchildren and so on up to seven generations will not be reborn in the lower realms. This is because your body is blessed by the mantra, and as their bodies are descended from yours, their bodies also carry these blessings, which affect their minds at the time of death and thus prevent them from being reborn in the lower realms. Even when a person who has recited that many mantras every day has died and is being cremated, the smoke coming from that special body purifies other sentient beings' karma. Whatever sentient beings—animals, insects, human beings—this smoke touches all get liberated from the lower realms by purifying their negative karma.

Now for the dedication. Due to these merits—all the past, present, and future merits—especially those arising from making prayer wheels, turning them, and making commentaries on the benefits available, as well as those arising from even seeing, remembering, or dreaming of prayer wheels or these benefits and instructions, may all those beings never be reborn in the lower realms from now on, and may all the disease, spirit harm, negative karma, and obscurations be completely purified immediately. May all their wishes succeed immediately according to holy Dharma, may they achieve full enlightenment as soon as possible, and especially may they actualize bodhichitta as quickly as possible. May they each become a source of all sentient beings' happiness, like the White Lotus of Great Compassion. And, may everyone who reads these benefits and does this very precious practice actualize the qualities more precious than the whole sky filled with jewels or billions of dollars and cause all sentient beings to achieve enlightenment as quickly as possible by purifying and collecting merit. So, from the heart, I offer my thanks to my dear students Lorne and Theresa, to all the readers, and to those who engage in the prayer wheel practice and inspire others.

Thank you very much.

Preface

ॐIn Mahayana Buddhism,[1] when holy beings make vows to accomplish particular tasks for the sake of suffering beings, the effects are said to be inconceivable. By making and keeping such vows of compassion, it is said that a bodhisattva can even turn an ordinary environment into a pure land of a buddha—an environment perfectly suited to helping others to progress toward enlightenment. Such a vow is something that cannot be turned back. In my own experience, I've sometimes felt that the vows of bodhisattvas are like ever-reliable springs, continually giving pure and refreshing water. At other times, I've felt that they are like the love of a mother for her child, indestructible regardless of circumstances. From a Mahayana Buddhist perspective, though, such similes inevitably fail because the vows of a bodhisattva go far beyond the benefits of this life; realized bodhisattvas like His Holiness the Dalai Lama commit absolutely to benefiting all beings, including oneself, throughout infinite time, regardless of what one does or what one becomes, never turning back or turning away until each being who suffers, again including oneself, is a fully realized, totally enlightened buddha.

For one not familiar with the world of Mahayana Buddhism, the expansive altruism and vast power of the bodhisattva way can be dizzying, like finding oneself suddenly in the high air and brilliant light of the Himalayas. I recall once explaining to a group of friends how bodhisattvas perfect their skill and wisdom in working for others across "countless" eons—time spans of so many millions of years, with so many zeros, that as I described them, we all became breathless. If a world of inconceivable wisdom and compassion is unfamiliar, though, it is also full of wonder; it is a place where the suffering find refuge and where the loving heart is at home. I mention all of this because, according to tradition, by spinning a prayer wheel even once (and, perhaps to some extent, by reading the translations in this book), one is connecting oneself with the vast vows of the buddhas—touching or entering a river that flows to the ocean of enlightenment.

Most prayer wheels are filled with many copies of the mantra of Avalokiteshvara, the Buddha of Compassion: *Om mani padme hum.* So, much of the spiritual power of the prayer wheel derives from the power of his mantra, his compassionate realizations, and his past vows. One sutra says that his "universal vows are as deep as the ocean.... When people hear his name and see his body and think of him...not vainly, they will see every form of ill effaced in all the worlds."[2] By connecting with the prayer wheel, one is connecting with the energy of Avalokiteshvara and with the Buddhist masters through the ages who transmitted this practice. One is connecting with an outer manifestation of enlightened compassion and awakening one's own highest potential, one's buddha nature.

I myself first became interested in the prayer wheel in connection with a vow that my teacher, Lama Thubten Zopa Rinpoche, made. It was 1991, and I had traveled to Nepal with my wife Theresa, who I married during the trip. We'd gone to Asia to make a pilgrimage to a number of Buddhist holy sites and then to visit Kopan Monastery in Nepal where Lama Zopa Rinpoche was to teach for a month.

The first time I can recall turning a prayer wheel was during our pilgrimage at the Great Stupa of Boudhanath in the Kathmandu valley of Nepal. Boudhanath is an ancient holy place; the Great Stupa sits, majestic as the Buddha himself. Serene Buddha-eyes painted on each of the four sides of an upper level of the stupa seem to watch compassionately as prayer flags flutter, children scurry, Tibetan yogis meditate silently, tourists buy tea and Buddha statues from shopkeepers, and faithful pilgrims continually circumambulate while turning hand-held prayer wheels or any of the hundreds of metal prayer wheels that have been installed along the outer edge of the stupa.

On our first day or so in Boudhanath, I went to visit the monastery of His Eminence Chogye Trichen Rinpoche, one of the greatest living Tibetan meditation masters and a teacher to His Holiness the Dalai Lama. I'd met His Eminence a few years earlier when he'd visited the United States, and he'd told me to come visit him if I was ever in Nepal. His monastery formed part of the wall of buildings that surrounded the Great Stupa. We sat for a while listening to a teaching His Eminence was giving in Tibetan. The walls of the assembly hall were painted with beautiful portraits of lamas from the monastery's lineage. The room was crowded with Tibetan lamas, monks, and lay people. I remember that I was sitting next to a Tibetan who continually turned what looked like an ancient hand-held prayer wheel. Later, as we were leaving the monastery, I paused to peer into a darkened room just by the monastery gate. A middle-aged Tibetan father suddenly pointed at me. "Hey you," he called out, gesturing for me to enter. Inside was a giant, very beautiful prayer wheel; it must have stood eight or twelve feet high, with a diameter of five or six feet. It was turning slowly; the father seemed concerned about children who were trying to turn the wheel but were slipping. At his command, the children stepped back. He gestured for me to help and began turning the wheel. We got the wheel turning at a steady pace. With each rotation, a bell on the ceiling rang. The children laughed and Theresa smiled.

Soon after this, we made our way up to Kopan Monastery, which sits atop a hill overlooking the Great Stupa, and from where one can see the Himalayas in the distance. Lama Zopa Rinpoche is a Sherpa—a cultural group from the Mount Everest region of Nepal who have long practiced Tibetan Buddhism. Sherpas are well known in the West for their part in expeditions to the summit of Mount Everest. During his month of teachings, Lama Zopa Rinpoche showed great patience and care as he led hundreds of students from around the world through the vast and profound passes and marvelous peaks in the mountains of Buddhist thought.

Around the end of the first week, Theresa and I had the opportunity to meet privately with him one evening in his small room atop the temple. The atmosphere in this room where he meditated was otherworldly—very pure, so that I felt both calmer and more joyful than I could recall ever having felt previously. I was deeply struck by Rinpoche's great kindness and mindfulness during our meeting. Although he himself was fasting, he offered us a number of drinks and gourmet snacks not easy to find in Nepal, while answering our many questions. I recall at one point his stopping to have Theresa help him move a small insect from the floor where he feared it might get stepped on—as the Buddha taught: Harm not a single living being.

Late that evening, Lama Zopa Rinpoche began talking to us about prayer wheels. He explained that as a young boy he'd often wondered why so many older people spun prayer wheels. He told us the story of his long search for a text on the benefits of this practice and of how he'd eventually found a lama who had such a text. The text that this lama lent to him is the first of the translations that appear in this book. Lama Zopa Rinpoche explained that on reading this text and understanding the benefits of this practice, he had placed the text atop his head and vowed to Avalokiteshvara, the Buddha of Compassion, that he would spread this practice everywhere.

I was intrigued by this story Rinpoche had shared, and the next day I mentioned it to my sister, who was in Nepal as an exchange student and was also attending the course at Kopan. A few days later, she bought me a small, hand-held prayer wheel. When Lama Zopa Rinpoche saw me trying to turn the wheel, he came over and very patiently showed me the correct way to turn it—upright, smoothly and steadily. Theresa was standing next to me, and he again told us about the text he'd found, about the remarkable benefits of the prayer wheel, and about his vow to the Buddha of Compassion. Suddenly, without much forethought about how we might go about doing so, I blurted out, "Theresa and I will help." Lama Zopa Rinpoche said, "When you read of the benefits, you'll want everyone to have one."

I think that one thing that inspired me to want to help was my awareness that Lama Zopa Rinpoche had made this vow to spread this practice while also making and fulfilling countless other vows and commitments for the sake of others. If I didn't actually know people like Lama Zopa Rinpoche, I probably wouldn't believe they existed. Those who live and travel with him say that he appears almost never to sleep and rarely even lies down. He is continually teaching, meditating, praying, translating texts, writing to students, and working on countless projects to benefit others. Under his direction, hospices care for the dying in numerous countries; leprosy and tuberculosis are being eliminated in Bodhgaya, India; free food is being provided to thousands of refugee monks from Tibet; a statue of the future Buddha Maitreya—the largest metal statue in the world—is being built in India; hundreds of other statues, stupas, and paintings are being made; books are being published; schools, Buddhist centers, and monasteries are being run. Listing the activities he is currently involved in would require an entire book. So, when he mentioned this particular vow he'd made, I felt inspired to help in some small way with this one among many projects.

After returning to the U.S., Theresa and I began making free-standing, wooden prayer wheels that were just under a foot high to give to friends, Buddhist centers, and lamas we knew. Despite my poor skills as an artisan, I've repeatedly been struck by people's comments about the benefits they've experienced from such prayer wheels. A number of times, years after receiving a prayer wheel, a friend would call or write to say that when going through some difficulty, turning the prayer wheel had helped them get back in touch with their own inner spiritual vision and ability to meditate. Others have noted how large prayer wheels have helped improve the energy in meditation centers. Years ago, my wife took a prayer wheel I'd given her as a wedding gift to a beauty shop where she worked, and months later when she left her job there, the owner and other workers, who were not Buddhist, begged her to leave it in the shop because of the "blessings and good energy" that they experienced from it.

While making prayer wheels, I also began asking Tibetan lamas about this practice and collecting what information I could about them. Though I haven't been able to help nearly as much as I would have liked, I have been amazed to watch as people in such varied places as Australia, Holland, Israel, India, France, Singapore, New Zealand, Nepal, Canada, and the U.S. have been inspired by Lama Zopa Rinpoche to build or obtain prayer wheels. When possible, I've tried to share some of the information I've gathered with such people, and it has been a great gift to be able to see some of the benefits described in the Tibetan commentaries arise in people's lives. It is my hope that this book will contribute in some way to fulfilling Lama Zopa Rinpoche's great vow.

I have often felt hesitant as I worked on this book because I am not a translator or Buddhist scholar. However, as I looked over the history of the prayer wheel practice, it became apparent that this practice was upheld mainly by great yogis and simple lay practitioners. It has not generally been popular in the great monastic universities of Tibet, and Western religious scholars have written very little on the subject. So, given that Lama Zopa Rinpoche, a great yogi in modern times is the force behind this book, I began to feel that it was not entirely unsuitable that a simple, Buddhist layman like myself should be involved in bringing it together. Particularly with regard to Part One, which I wrote myself, the intent is primarily to put the practice of the prayer wheel in context for readers who may be unfamiliar with the Mahayana Buddhist context, while also sharing some basic reflections on the nature and symbolism of this practice. I apologize to scholars and practitioners for any errors and sincerely hope that others will add to and clarify what is offered here.

Regarding the structure of the book itself, I see it as a series of circumambulations of the subject of the prayer wheel. This practice of circumambulating clockwise is an ancient one common to India and elsewhere. In some

Buddhist temples, there are routes for circumambulation that allow one to come closer to the subject with each round. One might say that this book is structured in this way.

As noted, the first part of this book attempts to put the practice of the prayer wheel in context. It includes some discussion of the place of this practice in relation to other practices, the lineage of the prayer wheel, and some aspects of its symbolism.

The second part of this book is really its heart. It contains sources from Tibetan masters, including an edited transcript of an oral discourse on the practice of the prayer wheel by Lama Zopa Rinpoche, and translations of all or part of a number of different Tibetan commentaries on the prayer wheel by Tibetan authors, including the Fourth Panchen Lama. This section will give readers the opportunity, for the first time, to access a collection of indigenous materials related to this practice.

The third part of the book takes us inside the prayer wheel itself, providing copies of the mantras and mandala-like wheels that prayer wheels are filled with, along with diagrams and pictures of how prayer wheels are constructed and decorated.

Finally, the fourth part of this book presents a meditation and visualization practice that one can use while turning a prayer wheel. It integrates the advice from the preceding commentaries into a structured format that can be put into practice.

Photos of prayer wheels are included with the text. I hope that these will give readers a general sense of the beautiful artistry with which Tibetans have built these sacred wheels. Lama Zopa Rinpoche also emphasized that including photos of particularly beautiful prayer wheels may be of use to craftsmen and artists who may wish to build prayer wheels in the future.

It is my sincere hope that this process of circumambulating the subject of the prayer wheel brings benefits in accord with the wishes, prayers, and vows of Lama Zopa Rinpoche, Avalokiteshvara, and all the buddhas and bodhisattvas.

Acknowledgments

ॐAs the source of the prayer wheel lineage is the Buddha of Compassion, it seems suitable to begin by thanking His Holiness the Fourteenth Dalai Lama, who so perfectly embodies enlightened compassion in our time.

I also wish to express my gratitude and sincere devotion to Venerable Lama Thubten Zopa Rinpoche, who provided the initial inspiration and the guidance and practical assistance without which this project would never have reached completion. It is my sincere prayer that this book contributes in some small way to his vast efforts on behalf of all beings.

Other lamas who should be acknowledged for their direct or indirect help include H. E. Chogye Trichen Rinpoche, Venerable Kirti Tsenshab Rinpoche, Venerable Ribur Rinpoche, Venerable Lati Rinpoche, Venerable Geshe Lama Lhundrup, Venerable Geshe Tsulga, Venerable Lama Pema Wangdak, Venerable Geshe Tsultrim Gyeltsen, Khamlung Tulku, Venerable Geshe Kelsang Wangdu, and Venerable Khenpo Phuntsok Tashi.

For their help with translations, thanks are due to Lori Cayton, Wilson Hurley, Yeshe Kedrup, Venerable Tsering Tuladhar (Tsen-la), Venerable Michael Lobsang Yeshe, Fabrizio Pallotti, David Molk, Samdrup Tsering, and to Ngawangthondup Narkyid, or "Kuno," for his very kind and generous assistance. Thanks to Professor Gregory Schopen for permission to quote from his unpublished manuscript. A special thanks to Dan Martin for allowing his translation to appear here and for sharing his own extensive research on the subject of the prayer wheel.

For their help with various aspects of this project, I would also like to offer thanks to Venerable Roger Kunsang, Venerable Roger Munroe, Venerable Paula Chichester, Jim McCann, Steven Vannoy, Sam Cassaro, Tom Ivory, Debra Ladner, Pema Wangdak, Jeffrey Woodard, Ian Kaminsky, Alex Campbell,

Annie Dillard, Buddhapalita, Robert Jones, Gerry Gomez, Kathy Wood, Kathryn Culley, Susan Meinheit at the Library of Congress, and the library research staff at Pacifica Graduate Institute. Thanks also to David Kittelstrom of Wisdom Publications for his help in the production process and to E. Gene Smith for his helpful comments and corrections in editing this book.

Thanks also to my parents, Ronnie Chase and Stephen Ladner. And, finally, a very special thanks to my partner in this work from the beginning, Theresa Ladner.

❧ PART ONE:

*Prayer Wheel Practice,
Symbolism, & Lineage*

Practice:
Seeing with Eyes of Compassion

&In general, the emphasis in Buddhism is quite clearly on *inner* training, on transforming one's mind. His Holiness the Dalai Lama has said that whether an action becomes a practice of Buddhism, of Dharma, is primarily dependent on the motivation and understanding of the person doing the action. Actions motivated by attachment, aversion, or ignorance, regardless of any external appearances, are simply not Buddhist practices. And actions done out of a sense of compassionate altruism, with a correct understanding of the nature of things, may properly be labeled Dharma practices, regardless of how they appear. Lama Zopa Rinpoche has pointed out that "only by knowing their motivation can you label people's actions holy Dharma or worldly [activity]"; he has also said, "everything—temporal and ultimate happiness, day-to-day problems, and the endless future sufferings of samsara—is dependent upon your own mind."[3]

So, with this strong emphasis on the mind and mental training, one may ask what role holy or sacred objects like prayer wheels play in Buddhist practice. In fact, from the earliest times, certain objects were recognized as sacred in Buddhism. For example, although the monk's robes and begging bowl are outer signs, they have long been revered as reminders of the monk's inner commitment to moral conduct and to traversing the path to enlightenment. And, before his death, the Buddha gave instructions that his remains should be placed in a stupa. Stupas containing the relics of holy beings have been built and revered by Buddhist practitioners ever since.

During a conversation about the prayer wheel with Lama Pema Wangdak, a Tibetan lama who lives and teaches in New York, he mentioned that "turning the wheel of prayer" was "similar to circumambulating a stupa." He went on to explain that "anything you do with a symbol of the body, speech, and mind of Buddha has a lasting impact on your soul or mind."

The Buddhist teachings on karma indicate that actions done in relation to holy beings or holy objects such as stupas or prayer wheels are particularly potent. Interactions with such people or objects leave a deep and lasting impression on the mind. The Mahayana Buddhist sutras go into detail in describing the remarkable benefits of relating to holy objects—to symbols of the Buddha's enlightened body, speech, and mind. For example, Shantideva, in his *Shiksasamuchaya*, quotes the *Avalokana Sutra* as follows:

> He who takes a speck smaller than a grain of mustard seed and burns incense on the Blessed One's shrines, hear me sing his praises and be your hearts serene, leaving obstinacy and sin. He...walks over all regions, altogether full of health, firm in mind, vigilant; he subdues pain, and walks in virtue, dear and beloved of the people.[4]

Understanding precisely how relating to an outer object such as a stupa or a prayer wheel can help one to train one's mind and to develop positive inner qualities is a very subtle and complex subject. When asked about how the blessing power of holy objects or holy beings benefits us, the great Tibetan master Lati Rinpoche explained how the power of the blessing depends not only on the power of the buddhas but also on one's own faith. He quoted a saying of the Kadampa lamas: "Big or small blessings don't depend on big or small lamas; it depends entirely on your level of perception and devotion." Similarly, a great young lama, Yangsi Rinpoche, likened the blessing power of the buddhas to a powerful crane, and faith to a hook or chain that allows the crane to lift up a large block of concrete: regardless of the crane's power, it cannot lift the concrete without that chain or hook.

It is said that the Buddha's mind—his omniscient, mental body of truth—is everywhere simultaneously. However, because of our ignorance, obscurations, and negative karma, we cannot perceive the Buddha's mental body. And similarly, it is said that even were the Buddha to emanate a shower of pure bodies, we would be unable to perceive them; we are like upside-down pots, which cannot catch even a drop of such a sacred rain. So, it would seem that through the force of their compassion, skillful means, and past vows, the buddhas must manifest in whatever forms beings can relate to. The most holy and important of all manifestations of the omniscient truth body of the buddhas are teachers of Dharma—gurus or lamas—who, by teaching the path to enlightenment, actually help beings to train their minds, so that they may purify negative tendencies, accumulate merit and positive tendencies, and gain realizations. The buddhas also manifest as holy objects—scriptures, statues, stupas, and prayer wheels—again in order to help beings to purify negativity, collect virtue, and gain realizations. One might say that these holy objects are like hooks, and by relating to them we connect ourselves with the powerful crane of the buddhas' qualities, allowing ourselves to be lifted up.

One other point on how holy objects like prayer wheels help one to develop positive qualities in the mind is worth noting here. Buddhist teachings emphasize how everything comes into being based on causes and conditions. And success in developing positive inner qualities clearly depends on many causes and conditions, including environmental factors. One Tibetan analogy notes that when a clean cloth is placed over a dung heap, it will gradually come to smell like dung, while another cloth placed over incense will come to smell very nice. Similarly, the environment in which practitioners (particularly those who are not yet highly realized) place themselves can have a powerful impact on their minds. For anyone interested in meditation, this is not a difficult point to prove for oneself experientially. (I need only compare my experience of trying to meditate during a week-long business trip to Las Vegas with my meditations during a week of group retreat led by a monk in a Buddhist center in Northern Vermont, to clarify this point for myself.) Many people have noted how having a prayer wheel near them helps them to meditate more effectively or to more easily develop positive states of mind. Though Tibetans may begin engaging in the prayer wheel practice based on faith, I suspect that most continue to engage in it based on their own experience of its leading to more peaceful, joyful, and virtuous mental states. This is certainly true of those practitioners I have spoken with over the years. A number of Tibetan commentaries state that having a prayer wheel in a building makes that place become like the Potala, the pure land of the Buddha of Compassion. It would seem that just as great yogis can perceive Buddha statues giving teachings or can see hidden pure realms, so also can they directly perceive the actual Potala pure land manifesting around a prayer wheel. Indeed, from talking with those who engage in this practice, it appears that by relating to a prayer wheel, even quite ordinary people can gain glimpses of that pure energy which is like otherworldly light shining through the veils of our ordinary perceptions.

Meditation and the Prayer Wheel

If part of the purpose or nature of the prayer wheel is to connect us with the buddhas and make the environment conducive to practicing virtue, it is only natural that meditating in connection with the prayer wheel will enhance the positive results.

It seems to me that the meditation practice suggested in the commentaries is very profound, combining important elements of Sutrayana and Mantrayana (or Vajrayana) Buddhist practice.[5] The prayer wheel practice is designed to simultaneously engage one's "three doors"—body, speech, and mind—in virtue. With one's body, one turns the prayer wheel. With one's speech, one recites the mantra of Avalokiteshvara. And with one's mind, one engages in specific contemplations and visualizations.

Part Four of this book, "A Method for Meditating with the Prayer Wheel," presents a structured meditation practice for use with the prayer wheel based on the Tibetan commentaries and on comments by Lama Zopa Rinpoche. The specific sufferings mentioned for each of the six realms of existence are derived from the traditional descriptions in the stages of the path [Tib. *lamrim*] literature. Those familiar with meditations from the Mantrayana or Vajrayana tradition of Mahayana Buddhism will note that a number of aspects of these meditations, such as the recitation of mantras and the visualization of light beams for the purification and enlightenment of all sentient beings, are included in this meditation. Many essential meditation subjects from the general Mahayana tradition are also included. For example, while engaging in this structured meditation, one contemplates such subjects as the sufferings of the three lower realms, the sufferings of samsara in general, the faults of the six root delusions, the four immeasurables (love, compassion, equanimity, and joy), and *bodhichitta*, the noble mind that aspires to full enlightenment for the benefit of all sentient beings.

In addition, the prayer wheel meditation is structured in a manner similar to the powerful mind training [Tib. *lojong*] technique called taking and giving [Tib. *tonglen*] which gives rise to great compassion and bodhichitta.[6] When doing the meditation of taking and giving, one begins by generating equanimity, love, and very strong compassion, and then one imagines taking all the sufferings of all sentient beings upon oneself. This is the practice of taking. What one is taking from others in this case is their suffering and its causes—their negative karmas, disturbing thoughts, and obscurations. This kind of taking derives from and enhances one's compassion, which is defined as the wish to free others from suffering. In the taking-and-giving meditation, one imagines drawing into oneself in the form of dark smoke all this negativity of others, destroying the self-cherishing (or narcissistic) thoughts that abide in one's heart. The great lama Pabongka Rinpoche says to "visualize all their suffering being shed like hair shaved off with a razor and taking the form of black rays that dissolve into the self-cherishing at your heart."[7]

One next engages in the meditation on giving, which is based on and enhances one's feelings of love, or the wish for others' happiness. Here, one visualizes giving away everything good that one has—one's possessions, body, knowledge, wisdom, and positive karma—to others, bringing them great happiness. Though such visualizations do not, on their own, remove others' sufferings or bring them happiness, it has been the experience of great Buddhist yogis over many centuries that this meditation does give rise over time to great inner qualities of love, compassion, inner strength, bravery, and bodhichitta. And these qualities in turn make one capable of progressing quickly toward full enlightenment so that one can actually provide the benefits that one formerly visualized.

In the prayer wheel meditation, one visualizes in turn each of the six realms of existence—realms of hell beings, hungry ghosts, animals, humans, demigods, and gods—and in each case one begins by visualizing taking away all of the sufferings, negative karmas, disturbing thoughts, and obscurations of all the beings in that realm. As in taking and giving, one begins with taking, enhancing one's feelings of compassion. The primary difference between this visualization and the visualization in the general taking-and-giving meditation is that here, rather than visualizing the dark cloud of negativity coming into oneself, one visualizes it being drawn into the prayer wheel, where it is completely destroyed. And, in the meditation on giving, rather than just visualizing giving away one's positivity, one visualizes giving all beings the infinite virtues and qualities of the Buddha of Compassion, which radiate in beams of light and touch all beings in each of the six realms, bringing them to full enlightenment. Thus, the prayer wheel meditation is a very practical means for enhancing one's love, compassion, and bodhichitta.

The prayer wheel meditation in Part Four is included to give the general reader a sense of how one would go about meditating with the prayer wheel. For those interested in actually doing the practice, it is designed so that it can be xeroxed for easy use.

Mantra Recitation & the Prayer Wheel

It is suggested that one recite the six-syllable mantra—*Om mani padme hum*—while turning the prayer wheel. The Tibetan commentaries state that the benefits of doing so are immeasurable. This is the mantra of Avalokiteshvara, the Buddha of Compassion, and it is recited continually by many Tibetans. One also finds it carved on rocks, written on prayer flags, embossed on jewelry, and inside of most prayer wheels. Among Tibetans it is commonly known as the *mani mantra,* and thus prayer wheels are often referred to among Tibetans as *mani wheels.*

Mantras are strings of syllables empowered by enlightened beings to benefit others. "The word 'mantra' means 'mind-protection.' It protects the mind from ordinary appearances and conceptions" that characterize the ongoing cycle of samsaric suffering.[8] Different mantras are said to bring different benefits, and many are kept secret and only revealed to students who have received initiation into a particular meditation practice. However, with regard to the mani mantra, Kalu Rinpoche notes that it "is extremely powerful" and "can be used by one and all" to speed their path to enlightenment.[9] His Holiness Dilgo Khyentse Rinpoche wrote, "The *mani* is not just a string of ordinary words. It contains all the blessings and compassion of [Avalokiteshvara]," and so he advises us to listen to this mantra, "recite it, read it, and write it beautifully in golden letters. Since there is no difference between the deity himself and the mantra which is his essence, these activities will bring great benefit."[10]

The role of mantras in Buddhist practice is often not well understood in the West. It has been scientifically documented that mantra recitation produces significant psychological and physiological relaxation,[11] and statistical analyses have shown that meditation with traditional mantras produces a greater reduction in anxiety than other kinds of meditation (including meditation with randomly selected Sanskrit syllables or with personally selected English words).[12] Westerners have tended to emphasize the relaxing effect of mantra recitation in their understanding of this practice. From a Tibetan Buddhist perspective, such relaxation is not the goal of mantra recitation; rather, it is a positive but minor side effect.

Kalu Rinpoche has explained how fully enlightened buddhas and highly realized bodhisattvas (those who have realized at least the eighth bodhisattva level) can perceive "sacred letters" within the *nadis* or energy channels of the subtle body.[13] He notes that such highly realized beings imbue mantras with specific powers, such as the ability to bring about health, increase intelligence, provide protection, and the like. Lama Thubten Yeshe has noted how the mantra of Vajrasattva has the power to purify negative karma. He describes how daily recitation of this mantra with clear concentration can stop negative karmas from increasing and how ongoing recitation with good concentration and insight "will be tremendously effective in eradicating impure concepts and the darkness of emotional obstacles."[14] Lama Zopa Rinpoche has often taught specific mantras that, if recited to beings at the time of death, have the power to stop them from taking lower rebirths and to cause them to gain good rebirths and to progress along the path to enlightenment. Some of these mantras are primarily meant to be recited, while others are designed to benefit others by being recited, written on prayer flags, written above the doors to houses, or rolled inside of stupas or statues. The descriptions of the benefits of such mantras are often similar to the benefits described in the texts on the prayer wheel.

Ultimately, the subject of mantras and of how they function in Buddhist practice is extremely vast and profound. What is important to understand here is that a mantra is not like a prayer *to* a divine being. Rather, the mantra—whether recited, written, or spun—*is* the deity, is enlightenment, immediately manifest. As Dilgo Khyentse Rinpoche says, "there is no difference between the deity himself and the mantra which is his essence."[15] Robert Thurman notes that when Tibetans recite the mani mantra, they are in effect saying, "All is well. Everything is perfect. Wisdom and compassion uphold every atom!"[16] In turning the prayer wheel and reciting the mani mantra, one is essentially attempting to put a full stop to the impure, samsaric world based on ignorance and self-centered attitudes. One is asserting with one's body, speech, and mind that the Buddha of Compassion is manifest here and now, that this is his pure land, and that the universe is completely filled with the brilliant light of compassionate wisdom, manifest everywhere in order to awaken beings.

With regard to the meanings of the mani mantra itself, it is said that not even a buddha could expound them all! One important point to understand is that *mani* is generally translated as "jewel" and *padme* is generally translated as "lotus." One common interpretation of the mantra is that these two symbolize method and wisdom respectively. That they are placed together indicates the necessity of practicing method and wisdom together in order to progress effectively toward enlightenment. The practitioner of the Mahayana

Buddhist path is sometimes likened to an eagle who needs two wings to fly; the bodhisattva flies to enlightenment on the wings of method and wisdom. His Holiness the Dalai Lama has written,

> Thus the six syllables, *om mani padme hum,* mean that in dependence on a path which is an indivisible union of method and wisdom, you can transform your impure body, speech, and mind into the pure exalted body, speech, and mind of a Buddha.[17]

It is generally explained that the syllable *om,* which is composed of three sounds—A, U, M—symbolizes the practitioner's impure body, speech, and mind, which will be purified through practice into the exalted body, speech, and mind of a buddha. His Holiness the Dalai Lama says that the syllable *hum* indicates indivisibility—that method and wisdom are generated as an indivisible unity in the mind of the Mantrayana practitioner.

Each of the six syllables can also be understood as corresponding to specific things to be purified or achieved. For example, they can be understood as corresponding to the six realms of existence (which must be purified), to the six root delusions (which must be overcome), and to the six kinds of veils (which must be purified). They can also be seen as corresponding to the six perfections to be completed on the path, to the six wisdoms to be realized, and to the six buddha families to be achieved. Table 1 gives some examples of correspondences that are directly relevant to the visualization practice of the prayer wheel.

Other texts list additional correspondences. For example, David Molk's translation of a teaching by the Tibetan king, Songtsen Gampo, says,

> Through reciting the six-syllable mantra one will attain the six siddhis. Through Om, one will attain the supreme siddhis; through Ma, the common siddhis; through Ni, the siddhi of pacifying sickness and spirits; through Pad, the siddhi to increase lifespan and merit; through Me, the siddhi to control people, wealth and food; and, through Hum, the siddhi to destroy enemies, obstructers and harmers.

Mantra Syllables	Tibetan Syllables	Colors	Six Realms Purified	Six Root Delusions	Six Perfections Completed
OM		White	Gods	Pride	Meditation
MA		Green	Demigods	Jealousy	Ethics
NI		Yellow	Humans	Desire	Joyous effort
PA		Blue	Animals	Ignorance	Wisdom
ME		Red	Hungry ghosts	Greed	Generosity
HUM		Indigo	Hell-beings	Anger	Patience

Table 1

This translation goes on to say,

> Through Om one will attain the body of Avalokiteshvara;
> through Ma, Avalokiteshvara's speech; through Ni, Avalokiteshvara's mind; through Pad, Avalokiteshvara's qualities; through
> Me, Avalokiteshvara's activity; and through Hum one will attain
> the deeds of Avalokiteshvara. Through Om one will attain the
> qualities of the path of accumulation; through Ma, qualities of
> the path of preparation; through Ni, qualities of the path of seeing; through Pad, qualities of the path of meditation; through Me
> one will attain the path of no more learning; and through Hum
> one will attain the qualities of omniscient mind. Thus, by reciting the six-syllable mantra, as soon as one passes away from this

life one will take birth in Sukhavati and, when Avalokiteshvara becomes the Buddha named Rasimamamudrata Srikutraraja one will be born miraculously from a lotus in His first retinue of disciples and attain the stage of irreversibility. Thus it is said.[18]

Clearly, the meaning of the mantra is multifaceted. In my own reflections, I've sometimes felt as though the mantra is a highly condensed, poetic expression through which enlightened beings share something of their inconceivable experience—a poetics of bliss, wisdom, and love. The primary way to benefit from the mantra is not by studying it, but by reciting it. As one can deepen one's understanding of a great poem by reading it over and over, one can deepen one's experience of the meaning and benefits of a mantra by reciting it many times. His Holiness Dilgo Kyentse Rinpoche has written,

> If you take the *mani* as your refuge both in happiness and in sorrow...[Avalokiteshvara] will always be with you, you will feel more and more devotion without any effort, and all by itself the realization of the Mahayana path will arise in your being.[19]

The Tibetan commentaries presented in this book state that by turning the prayer wheel and reciting the mani mantra, one's home becomes like the Potala pure land, and one becomes "equal in fortune to the Thousand Buddhas" and "meaningful to behold by anyone with whom one has a connection" so that even "sentient beings who are touched by one's shadow will be liberated from the lower realms."[19] Lama Zopa Rinpoche similarly describes how if one recites at least one thousand mani mantras per day, then one's body becomes blessed and benefits everyone who comes into contact with you. What is being suggested here is that by engaging in the practice of turning the prayer wheel and reciting the mani mantra, one actually becomes a point of connection for others to contact the energy of the enlightened. One's own body becomes, in some sense, like a holy place or like a stupa—a place where the Buddha's omniscient mental body of truth manifests for the benefit of others.

Watching my own and other people's reactions to such claims about the benefits of this practice has been interesting. From a modern, mechanistic view of reality, such benefits may seem implausible. But from a Buddhist perspective, where the power of the mind and the possibility of enlightenment are understood, such benefits are by no means inconceivable. The great yogi, Lama Thubten Yeshe, describes how in Vajrayana Buddhism, symbols and visualizations can be very powerful in "introducing us to our essential nature" which is divine and limitless.[20] He suggests that we remain horribly trapped by our own narrow and suffocating self-image, enslaved by the "tyranny of ordinary appearances and conceptions."[21] He says that Buddhist tantra challenges us to dissolve our claustrophobic, dissatisfied self-concept and open up to seeing ourselves "as transcendentally beautiful—as gods and goddesses in fact," thus recognizing "the fully awakened experience latent within us."[22]

In my experience, the prayer wheel has been an invitation to break free of the tyranny and narrowness of ordinary self-concepts, and a reminder that one can do so. Often when I feel discouraged or overly self-critical, I will remind myself to reread the descriptions of the benefits of the prayer wheel practice. At one point, Lama Zopa Rinpoche showed me how he had attached to his own prayer wheel a few handwritten pages of quotations about the benefits of the practice. This encouraged me to keep reminding myself to challenge self-limitations and to try to have the joy and audacity to see myself as capable of being of profound benefit and true service to others.

While contemplating these subjects, I happened to come across an interesting account in a book by Delog Dawa Drolma—a lama and visionary and the mother of Chagdud Tulku. The book describes her journey through various realms of existence during a near-death experience and is reminiscent of Dante's descriptions of his journeys through heaven and hell. On a number of occasions, particularly during her journeys through hell, she describes seeing various people turning a prayer wheel and sweetly singing the mani mantra or some prayer of compassion; and on such occasions, beings caught in the miseries of hell rise up and follow these people to pure lands. Once, a nun leads a thousand hell beings out of hell toward the pure land of the female Buddha, Tara. Dawa Drolma notes that the nun was able to do this because those beings "were connected to her through speech or touch."[23] That is, the nun who engaged in this practice was able to benefit those beings simply because each of them had touched her or heard her speak during his or her previous life.

When I was young, I was quite intrigued by Arthurian legends of heroes who searched for and found magical objects such as the Holy Grail and Excalibur, through which they could benefit others. The prayer wheel, which according to tradition was brought to the human realm by the great bodhisattva hero

Nagarjuna from the realm of the dragonlike *nagas*, is remarkable in part because it is a similarly magical or divine object that invites or, perhaps, dares one to finally see one's own divine, archetypal capacity for enlightened and magical compassion.

Symbolism:
The Radiant Dharma Wheel

&❦ One of the most universal symbols in the world, both in and out of the Buddhist context, is the wheel or circle as a solar emblem. One scholar asserts that "the concept of the sun as a wheel was one of the most widespread notions of antiquity."[24] This kind of symbolism was already present in India before the time of the Buddha, and it certainly influenced the understanding of the wheel as a symbol in Buddhism. Tibetan lama and scholar Dagyab Rinpoche has said regarding the wheel, "The circle…is a universal symbol found in all cultures. In pre-Buddhist India…[the wheel often served] as a symbol for the sun, or, derived from this, for time or any kind of cyclical motion."[25]

In the Indian tradition, the sun god Surya was pictured riding a chariot with just one wheel, symbolizing the orb of the sun and his staying on the one right or just path across the sky from east to west each day. The Indian Buddhist master, Chandragomin, who was known as a great devotee of the Buddha of Compassion, wrote of the bodhisattva's expansively compassionate motivation, specifically using imagery from Surya in his solar chariot:

> The Sun
> Climbs aboard his fantastic chariot,
> Flies across the sky,
> Lights up the world…
> And so is the way
> Of those great beings
> Who wish nothing
> For themselves,

Their lives devoted
To a single song:
The well-being and the happiness
Of every living thing.[26]

From early times, Surya was represented in statues by the solar wheel, and these statues are quite similar to Buddhist statues of the wheel of Dharma.[27] In India, there is a very ancient tradition regarding the wheel-turning king [Skt. *chakravartin*] that appears to be related to the religious understanding and imagery associated with Surya. The wheel here is a symbol of "universal dominion."[28] Apparently, the original meaning of the term "wheel-turning king" was that such a king was so powerful that he would gain dominion wherever he rode his great chariot. Thus, one might say that a wheel-turning monarch's rise to power occurs as naturally as the sun's rising and that he rules with a power like the all-important power and radiance of the sun.

The association of kings with solar imagery is a common theme in many cultures. Solar gods associated with sky-going chariots or wheels and with divine law, such as Surya and his Greek counterpart, Apollo, appear in many times and cultures. Even the Old Testament describes a vision of the prophet Ezekiel in which four bright, luminescent angels with animal faces, floated in a great, whirling cloud of fire, each accompanied by a mystical wheel that floated alongside him containing or expressing the spirit of the angel. Jewish Talmudic scholars understood the wheels of these unusual angels as the wheels of a celestial chariot, a chariot of God himself.[29] Thus is the symbolism of Ezekiel's vision linked with that of Surya and other solar deities.[30]

The wheel has always been an important symbol in Buddhism. The symbol of the wheel certainly played an important role throughout the life of the historical Buddha.

It is said that when the Buddha was born, his father—a king—asked a seer to predict his son's future. The young child had been born with a number of remarkable, auspicious signs on his body, including natural marks in the shape of wheels on the soles of his feet and on his palms. Such marks are among the thirty-two major marks or physical characteristics of a great being—the results of vast positive karma. The seer said that the Buddha-to-be had remarkable qualities; he would either become a wheel-turning king or become a buddha, a fully awakened being.

By the Buddha's time, the wheel of the wheel-turning king was no longer thought of primarily as part of a chariot, but had become one of the seven emblems of sovereignty. The *Cakkavatti Sihanada Sutta* describes how "this magnificent wheel appears in mid-air" before the wheel-turning king "at the beginning of his reign as a sign of his righteousness" and power.[31] One Tibetan text describes this "precious wheel" as being "as beautiful as a second sun in the world…in a single day, it rolls unhindered for a hundred thousand *yojana* through the sky….Wherever the Chakravartin wishes to go…he goes there in the sky with the aid of the thousand-spoked wheel."[32] As a young man, the Buddha had a choice: to become such a powerful, wheel-turning monarch or to leave his kingdom and enter into forest solitude to pursue deep meditation and seek the enlightenment of buddhahood. He chose to pursue this second course, and after years of meditation, he awakened to the true nature of things. Even a wheel-turning king is not free from the sufferings of illness, aging, loss, and death. From a Buddhist perspective, only enlightened wisdom can grant such freedom.

The Buddha renounced his option of becoming a wheel-turning monarch—the option of having unlimited worldly power. According to tradition, after the Buddha's enlightenment, he sat in silence for some time until the gods came to him and said: "Arise, O great ocean of compassion, and turn the holy wheel of Dharma."[33] Turning the wheel of Dharma refers to giving teachings on the truth, on the Buddhist path to enlightenment. The First Dalai Lama refers to the Buddha as a "self-born lord of truth" and a "Dharma king."[34] Thus, rather than becoming a worldly, wheel-turning king, he became a king of the realm of truth, who by turning the wheel of Dharma awakens others to the true nature of things.

A number of the Tibetan commentaries on the prayer wheel refer to turning the prayer wheel as "turning the Dharma wheel." One commentary says that by engaging in the practice of the prayer wheel, "one gains a connection to [a buddha's] turning of the wheel of Dharma." The Tibetan commentaries agree that the practice ultimately leads one to become a buddha—a lord of truth who turns the wheel of Dharma for others.

In my own reflections on this subject, I am reminded of the teachings on the four kinds of karmic results of actions. For a negative action such as killing, these could include the *ripened result* of rebirth in the lower realms, the *experience congruent with the cause* such as having a short life, the *action congruent with the cause* such as killing again in this or future lives, and the *environmental results* such as living in violent places. Though the karmic benefits of the prayer wheel practice are seemingly inconceivable, as one looks at specific benefits listed in the commentaries one finds that they do include these four kinds of karmic results. For example, ripening results may include rebirth as a human or god. Experiences congruent with the cause may include receiving those realizations and qualities that one has visualized radiating to others and receiving teachings—being present when a buddha turns the wheel of Dharma. Environmental results may include living in a pure and beautiful environment, like a pure land. Actions congruent with the cause may include having compassion in future lives, engaging in the prayer wheel practice again in future lives, and even turning the wheel of Dharma for others.

Though the specifics of how karma ripens is beyond the view of ordinary beings, it does seem that an awareness of the symbolism related to the wheel in the Buddhist tradition can be of value as one contemplates the meanings and benefits of prayer wheel practice. Thinking of these benefits may help one rejoice in positive actions and thereby increase their power.

Awareness of the symbolic resonances in the ritual of the prayer wheel may help one to understand what the ritual evokes. Just as the buddhas communicate with the conscious mind through teachings on subjects like impermanence, compassion, and emptiness, so also do they communicate with the subconscious through rituals and symbols to awaken hidden potentials.

Here I shall discuss how three archetypal qualities of solar symbolism appear to relate to the prayer wheel practice. This discussion reflects my own attempt as a modern Westerner to understand something that people of other times and cultures may have intuited directly. I hope this discussion may help others to understand what may be an unfamiliar language of symbolism. I do not claim, however, that these reflections are definitively valid in relation to the prayer wheel practice.

One kind of archetypal solar symbolism evoked by the prayer wheel is the timeless image of the sun as giving protection against the demonic forces of darkness. The Tibetan commentaries mention in a number of places that turning the prayer wheel protects one from evil powers, including demigods [Skt. *asuras*], harm-givers [*yakshas*], demons [*maras*], interferers, and "demonic planets." In ancient India and elsewhere, the sun was believed to "drive away darkness and demons from the gods in the sky as well as from the earth."[35] Solar divinities are also often believed to be able to dispel the effects of negative astrological conditions. The god Surya was frequently pictured (as in the Buddhist caves at Bhaja) riding his chariot and "destroying the evil powers of darkness, personified as demons."[36] However, while the Tibetan commentaries suggest that prayer wheel rituals can help to dispel these external negative forces, they make clear that the principle demons to be overcome through the practice are the inner, psychological demons such as self-centeredness, pride, anger, and ignorance. (Cf. the psychologist C.G. Jung's descriptions of how terrified he was when he faced the demons and demigods of his inner world.) On the difficult, inner journey through the darker regions of the soul, turning the prayer wheel can bring light, just as compassion can lighten the darkest sorrows.

Another kind of solar symbolism that the prayer wheel seems to invoke is the sun as a source of warmth, light, and growth. As the sun gives warmth and light to all beings on the earth and causes crops to grow, it may be seen as a symbol of goodness, well-being, and prosperity. Similarly, the Tibetan commentaries suggest that the prayer wheel can bring healing, wealth, and the like to the practitioner. However, the visualization practice makes it clear that as the emanation of light-beams from the prayer wheel reaches beings, it primarily causes Dharma realizations to grow. The sections of the Tibetan commentaries describing the visualizations to be done while turning the prayer wheel specifically mention visualizing beams of light emanating from the prayer wheel "striking migratory beings," causing them to "spontaneously develop the four immeasurable thoughts—loving-kindness, compassion, joy, and equanimity" and to "complete the practice of the six perfections—giving, morality, patience, perseverance, concentration, and wisdom." The language here is similar to some descriptions of the Buddha, such as this one, from the *Avatamsaka Sutra*:

> Having cultivated generosity, self-control, and patience,
> Diligence and meditation,
> And ultimate transcendent wisdom,
> With them he lights the world.[37]

The spiritual light of the Buddha in this sutra, like the spiritual light visualized emanating from the prayer wheel, has the particular character of inspiring the practice and completion of the six perfections, which comprise the heart of the bodhisattva's practice on the path to full enlightenment, or buddhahood. As one commentary says, through this practice, "the disciple will ripen like a good harvest."

A third kind of solar symbolism evoked for me by prayer wheel practice is the sun's westward transit across the sky each day as a symbol of the right path. That the prayer wheel is spun clockwise, just as stupas are generally circumambulated clockwise, seems to be related to this symbolism. In the Buddhist tradition, clockwise circumambulation is a sign of respect; a number of Buddhist sutras describe disciples doing three clockwise circumambulations of the Buddha and prostrating to him before requesting teachings. (The word *clockwise* is an adaptation of an earlier term translated from the Sanskrit as "sunwise.") Lama Govinda, writing of this custom of circumambulation, notes that at the great Buddhist stupa of Sanchi, "the orientation of the gates equally corresponds to the sun's course: to sunrise, zenith, sunset, nadir," with each of these four being associated with one of the Buddha's four major deeds: east for birth, south for enlightenment, west for setting in motion the wheel of Dharma, and north for his final liberation.[38] Thus, in circumambulating such a stupa, one is both paying homage to and symbolically following the life-course of the Buddha—following the right path.

It appears likely that our dual association with the word *right*—indicating one's right side and also indicating what is true, moral, and just—is associated with this ancient and archetypal idea of circumambulating clockwise, with one's right side to the center. William Simpson notes that the Sanskrit term *rita*, originally used to identify the "path followed every day by the sun from his rising to his setting," later came to mean "the eternal foundation of all that exists," the "law in general," and "all that is right, good, and true."[39]

Reflecting on how pervasive this archetypal idea of the auspiciousness of turning clockwise is, it is interesting to note how in our modern technology, we generally design objects so that locks, knobs, and faucets turn clockwise to let us in or turns things up or on.

So, through the simple gesture of turning a prayer wheel clockwise or circumambulating a holy object, one is evoking a very ancient and pervasive level of symbolism related to paying homage, to doing what is right, and to following a true and enlightening path.

Before concluding this section on symbolism, I want to say a few words about the symbolic quality of the inner structure of the prayer wheel. According to a number of Tibetan commentaries, in the center of the prayer wheel, one places a "life-tree" or central shaft upon which a number of sacred syllables and mantras are written. This is similar in design to the life-tree placed in the center of stupas. At the top and bottom of the prayer wheel, one then places mandala-like designs, which also have sacred syllables and mantras written on them. Both designs have a six-petaled lotus near the center, with each petal corresponding to a syllable of the mani mantra. The design placed at the bottom is called the "earth wheel," and the one at the top is called the "sky wheel."

The Tibetan word for mandala is *kyilkor*, which means "center and surrounding environment."[40] While the Tibetan commentaries do not explicitly mention this term, the Tibetan tradition does understand the mantra of Avalokiteshvara to be an actual manifestation of his omniscient mind. So, it is appropriate to consecrate the center and surrounding environment of the interior of the prayer wheel before inviting Avalokiteshvara himself to dwell in the prayer wheel by winding the mani mantras around the life-tree.

In concluding this section, I should note that while reflecting on the symbolism of a spiritual practice is important, it is also important to recall that, particularly in Buddhism, symbols are intended to point toward experiences that transcend symbolism. As the *Avatamsaka Sutra* says,

> The spiritual powers of the enlightening beings are also
> inconceivable.
> Though one may try to illustrate this by metaphor,
> After all there is no metaphor that can be likened to this;
> However, people of wisdom and intelligence
> Understand their meaning by means of similitudes.[41]

In a similar vein, with regard to the meaning of the Buddhist stupa, His Holiness the Dalai Lama has said that "the actual stupa exists in the heart center in each of us."[42] By means of symbolism, ritual, devotion, and practice, one may find the radiant prayer wheel of enlightened, universal compassion in one's own heart.

Lineage:
An Ancient & Mystical Inheritance

& Because Mahayana Buddhism views the spiritual careers of bodhi-sattvas as taking place over the course of eons and involving visits to various realms of existence, the Buddhist view of history is quite different from that of modern Western society. For example, it is said that in a previous eon, the being who would later become Shakyamuni Buddha met a buddha named Dipankara to whom he made offerings and in whose presence he generated the wish to become a buddha himself. According to a number of Tibetan commentaries, this inconceivably ancient buddha held the lineage of the prayer wheel and gave it to the *nagas*[43] (powerful, long-lived serpents or dragonlike beings who usually live in oceans or other deep bodies of water and have the ability to magically take on human appearance). The particular nagas to whom Dipankara Buddha gave the prayer wheel lineage were Mahayana Buddhist practitioners, and their king was a bodhisattva. The commentaries suggest that over the course of millions of years, these nagas used the prayer wheel and many attained high levels of realization on the path to enlightenment.

It is never suggested that Dipankara Buddha originated the prayer wheel practice, so one gets a sense of a lineage of compassion reaching back limitlessly across eons. The celestial Buddha of Compassion, Avalokiteshvara, is also associated with the prayer wheel lineage, but the commentaries do not indicate that he began the lineage either. Trying to relate the modern Western view of history—which focuses almost exclusively on the past few thousand years—to the Buddhist view can at times feel like comparing a detailed street map of one's neighborhood to a map of the galaxies: the scale is so radically different. Understanding the Buddhist tradition's view of lineage can give one a sense of touching something timeless and remind one of the expansive bodhisattva world-view from which the prayer wheel practice comes.

Texts suggest that the prayer wheel lineage remained with the nagas for millions of years until the time of Nagarjuna, a famous Indian Buddhist scholar, philosopher, and yogi. Nagarjuna is associated with the rise of Mahayana Buddhism during the first century B.C.E. and is known as the founder of the Middle Way school of Buddhist philosophy, which all currently existing schools of Tibetan Buddhism accept as the most profound of all philosophical views and which was the wellspring for the Ch'an and Zen traditions of China and Japan as well.

Because Nagarjuna is so important in the lineage of the prayer wheel, it may be worthwhile to look at the Buddhist tradition's understanding of who he was. It is believed that during the time of the Buddha, the one who would later take birth as Nagarjuna was reborn as a youth named Priyadarshana, who was a student of the great lay Buddhist sage Vimalakirti. During a famous teaching by Vimalakirti on nonduality, this youth achieved a high level of insight. "The Buddha subsequently predicted that this young man would be reborn in South India four hundred years later"[44] as one "who would spread his central way teaching far and wide, and then go on to the pure land of Sukhavati; and that he would be called 'Naga.'"[45] That Shakyamuni Buddha predicted Nagarjuna would eventually be reborn in the pure land of Sukhavati—the "land of bliss"—is of interest, as this is the pure land of the Buddha Amitabha, the celestial guru of Avalokiteshvara. Also, a number of commentaries on the prayer wheel translated in this book say that one who engages in the practice of the prayer wheel will take rebirth precisely in this pure realm, Sukhavati.

Although not all scholars agree on Nagarjuna's dates, it appears that he was born around the first century B.C.E. in southern India. While still a boy, he took ordination as a monk and entered Nalanda monastic university, the greatest university in India at that time. There, he studied the Buddha's teachings and India's arts and sciences, proving himself an extremely capable young scholar.[46] He remained at Nalanda for many years and became famous as a teacher. He is also said to have become a student of the great tantric adept, Saraha. While studying and teaching the exoteric Buddhist teachings, he apparently also engaged in practices of the esoteric Buddhist tantras and became a powerful alchemist as well.

One account of Nagarjuna's life says that even though he was already a great meditator and scholar, he would lie awake at night thinking, "I am use-less to other people in my present state of attainment. I must gain the capac-ity to help others."[47] In one of his later writings, *The [Two] Collections for Enlightenment*, Nagarjuna wrote,

> To recite for oneself and to teach others the profound scriptures praised by the Buddha, and to explain the various meanings...To follow [the Buddha] and to turn the victorious *dharmacakra* turned by the Buddha,[48] and to calm and quench bad impulses—this is a bodhisattva's store of merit. By bearing the great suffer-ing of hell—not to mention a little extra suffering—so as to benefit and please living beings—*bodhi*[49] will be in the right hand. To initiate action not for oneself but only to benefit and please living beings, motivated by compassion—bodhi is in the right hand. Wisdom without conceptualization, zeal without sloth, generosity without stinginess—bodhi is in the right hand.[50]

Nagarjuna also wrote,

> May I be as dear to sentient beings as their
> Own life, and may they be very dear to me,
> May their sins fructify for me
> And all my virtues for them.[51]

It is clear from Nagarjuna's writings that he was someone filled with great compassionate concern for others. He was an extremely gifted and intelli-gent man who thought continually about how best to benefit others. The tra-ditional story says that, attracted by Nagarjuna's compassion and intelligence, the nagas took human form to invite Nagarjuna to their kingdom, where they held many Buddhist teachings that Shakyamuni Buddha himself had entrusted to their care until humans were ready to receive them.[52] Since the Buddha had predicted that Nagarjuna's name would include "naga," one may infer that the Buddha had entrusted these teachings to the nagas so that Nagarjuna might later transmit them to the human realm and there dissem-inate them.

There, under the sea, in the kingdom of the nagas, Nagarjuna received the Buddhist teachings that make up the heart of Mahayana Buddhism: the

Perfection of Wisdom, Lotus, Pure Land, Jewel Heap, Mission to Lanka, and *Inconceivable Liberation Sutras,* and many others.[53] Nagarjuna is said to have made numerous journeys to the nagas' kingdom and to have written and taught extensively on the sutras he discovered. Nagarjuna's teachings not only began one of the greatest philosophical traditions of all time, but also contributed immeasurably to a cultural transformation that spread the Mahayana Buddhist vision of universal responsibility and radical compassion through most of Central and East Asia.

A number of commentaries on the prayer wheel translated here indicate that Nagarjuna saw in a pure vision Avalokiteshvara, who instructed him to go to the king of the nagas and request a prayer wheel that had been given to the nagas long before by Dipankara Buddha. Avalokiteshvara told Nagarjuna that if he did this, "the benefits to sentient beings will be enormous."

In the Indian Mahayana tradition, others besides Nagarjuna had visionary encounters with Avalokiteshvara. The great Indian master Chandragomin is said to have been tutored in his debate with Chandrakirti by visionary discussions with Avalokiteshvara, and the Indian nun, Lakshmi, is said to have become highly realized after seeing Avalokiteshvara directly and receiving teachings and empowerments.[54] Also, Taranatha, in his *History of Buddhism in India,* describes how one friend of Nagarjuna's did a twelve-year retreat chanting the mantra of Avalokiteshvara and subsequently saw Avalokiteshvara directly and received from him supernatural powers allowing him to work effectively for the benefit of others.[55]

That the prayer wheel lineage is thus associated with both Nagarjuna and Avalokiteshvara suggests that it is an important symbol of Mahayana Buddhism. Indeed, the lineage of the prayer wheel in one form or another spread to most Mahayana Buddhist countries.

Over the past hundred years, Western scholars have debated whether the prayer wheel originated in India, Tibet, or China. Extant Tibetan commentaries are unanimous in their assertion that the practice came from India to Tibet. Without going into the anthropological and archaeological details, suffice it to say that I have found no compelling evidence to contradict the Tibetan claim. The symbolism of this practice clearly appears to be based on Indian imagery, and the Tibetan commentaries quote numerous sources that evince translation from the Sanskrit. Furthermore, in at least two instances, respected scholars refer to evidence that prayer wheels existed in northern India around the eleventh century. The first appears in Taranatha's history of the Tara tantra. This text indicates that, northeast of Bodhgaya, a group of Sinhalese *shravakas* burned a number of texts, destroyed a large statue, and "did great damage to the *Dharma-cakra* [Dharma-wheel] of Master Buddha-sri-jnana."[56] Martin Willson, the translator of this text, notes that Geshe Jampa Tekchok believes that this reference to a damaged Dharma-wheel probably refers to "a rotating wheel containing mantras, like a Tibetan prayer-wheel, possibly water driven."[57] The second reference occurs in a yet unpublished manuscript by Professor Gregory Schopen, who notes that an eleventh-century inscription at the site of Nalanda University (where Nagarjuna studied) refers to a device like a prayer wheel. The passage is part of a series of verses praising the good works of a monk named Vipulashrimitra. As translated by Schopen, the passage reads:

> From continuous effort (a copy of) the Mother of the Buddhas
> [the *Perfection of Wisdom Sutra*] constantly revolves in the great
> temple of the Holy Khasarppana [Avalokiteshvara], by means of
> the book case constructed by him [Vipulashrimitra], and he
> installed four images in the alms-houses on the holiday.

The reference seems to indicate that in a temple dedicated to Avalokiteshvara, this monk built a prayer wheel containing the *Perfection of Wisdom Sutra*. These two references to prayer wheels in India support the traditional Tibetan view of its history.

Although the majority of prayer wheels contain mani mantras, many variations have arisen. The mention of the prayer wheel containing a copy of the *Perfection of Wisdom Sutra* suggests that these variations began early in the tradition.

One important variation, which exists primarily outside of Tibet, is the revolving bookcase. Designed like prayer wheels, these revolving libraries or bookcases are large, turning cases, usually octagonal in shape (reminiscent of the eight-spoked Dharma wheel), and are turned clockwise on a central axis. Here, as in the case of the mani wheel, the suggestion is that by turning the wheel one creates virtuous karma comparable to that which one would create by reading or reciting the texts within. Revolving libraries have been found in China since the sixth century; whereas, the first references to the prayer wheel in Tibet appear to be during King Songtsen Gampo's reign in the seventh century. From China, revolving libraries spread to Korea, Japan, and other parts of East Asia.[58] By the eighth and ninth centuries, they had become quite popular in China. Padmasambhava, who according to tradition, transmitted the prayer wheel lineage to Tibet, did not arrive there until the eighth century.[59] Although the first revolving libraries probably came to China from India,[60] the available Chinese sources on this lineage are currently quite limited.[61] One Tibetan commentary says that "Nagarjuna asked his benefactor, a Dharma king, to make a wheel containing the canon of Buddha's teachings to be turned." If this Tibetan text is correct, then the tradition of the revolving bookcase was begun by Nagarjuna.

In the Tibetan tradition, it is acceptable to fill prayer wheels with mantras and prayers of buddhas other than the Buddha of Compassion or, in some cases, to include the mantras of a number of different buddha deities in one prayer wheel. One Tibetan commentary states that a yogi named Mingtangpa had a pure vision of Lama Tsongkhapa regarding building a prayer wheel filled with the *migtsema*, a praise to Tsongkhapa. While traveling in Asia, my wife Theresa and I have seen prayer wheels of the Buddha Kalachakra (associated with the mystical kingdom of Shambhala) and of the Buddha Vajrasattva (associated with purification). In Dharamsala, India, there are prayer wheels of several buddha deities, including a female buddha named Sitatapatra, or "White Umbrella." Finally, some lamas in America are overseeing the construction of prayer wheels containing Padmasambhava's mantra.

A number of Tibetan lamas have indicated that it is acceptable to build prayer wheels with other prayers inside. Under the direction of Tarthang Tulku, the Yeshe De Project in California made a large number of hand-held prayer wheels containing forty-two different texts and prayers.[62] A Western Buddhist once asked Lama Zopa Rinpoche if it would be beneficial for her to make a prayer wheel containing her favorite Buddhist text, the *Essence of True Eloquence* by Lama Tsongkhapa. Lama Zopa Rinpoche replied that it would be beneficial, but he could not guarantee that it would be as beneficial as a mani wheel.

I asked Venerable Geshe Gyaltsen, a Tibetan lama who has been living and teaching in Los Angeles for many years, about using different mantras in a prayer wheel. He assured me that it was acceptable to use mantras other than the mani mantra in prayer wheels or even to mix several mantras in the same prayer wheel, though he did advise against mixing prayers from different religions. Lama Pema Wangdak in New York agreed that it was acceptable to make prayer wheels containing numerous mantras and suggested that particular configurations of mantras might be especially beneficial, for example, placing the mani mantra in the center, Manjushri's mantra in the middle, and Vajrapani's mantra outside of that.[63] He also proposed a prayer wheel with the mantras of each of the deities [Tib. *yidam*] with whom one has a connection inside, arranging them from the inside out according to the traditional system shown in images of the lineage tree. The Tibetan tradition is not entirely consistent on this point; in one Tibetan commentary (reviewed by Dan Martin), the Sengchen Lama "voices his disapproval of the practice of putting more than one sacred text inside the same prayer wheel."[64] I spoke about this issue with Lama Zopa Rinpoche who advised me that while it is permissible to put copies of other deities' mantras in a prayer wheel, it is most beneficial to use primarily copies of the mani mantra.

According to Tibetan tradition, Nagarjuna passed the prayer wheel lineage on to a *dakini* (a female, angel-like being) with the face of a lion. Thus one gets the impression that the practice is primarily a mystical one of powerful, divine beings, only temporarily loaned, through the kindness of the Buddha of Compassion, to some fortunate members of humanity.

Even the Tibetan accounts of the human lineage holders contribute to this sense of a lineage transmitted by superhuman beings. According to Lama Zopa Rinpoche, the prayer wheel practice was never popular at the great monastic universities of Tibet. And yet, the greatest yogis of India and Tibet adopted it. After the eighth-century Indian master Padmasambhava brought the lineage to Tibet, it was later practiced by the Indian tantric Buddhist masters Tilopa and Naropa. Naropa's disciple Marpa later renewed the lineage in Tibet and passed it on to that renowned Tibetan meditator, Milarepa. Though these masters were of specific times and places—their historicity is not in doubt—each, through the power of his yogic realizations and inspiring deeds, is an almost mythic figure in Tibetan Buddhism. It was the great yogis, then, who disseminated the prayer wheel lineage in Tibet. Among these was the Kagyu master Karma Pagshi, whose works are quoted by most subsequent writers on the subject.

According to *The Blue Annals*, a great yogi and *siddha* of the fifteenth century named Sherab Pel engaged in the practice of the mani wheel.[65] In the seventeenth century, the great Gelugpa yogi scholar Losang Chokyi Gyaltsen built many mani wheels in the area of Tashi Lhunpo Monastery, as did Jetsun Losang Yeshe. In the nineteenth century, the great yogi Shabkar, whose autobiography stands beside Milarepa's as a favorite of Tibetans, also built mani wheels for the benefit of others in his later life.[66.] Even in modern times, one finds that it is yogis like His Eminence Chogye Trichen Rinpoche, His Holiness Trijang Rinpoche, Geshe Rabten, Lama Zopa Rinpoche, Chagdud Tulku, Geshe Lama Konchog (who spent over twelve years meditating in strict retreats in the caves of Milarepa), and other yogis from the various Tibetan traditions who teach this practice and inspire the building of prayer wheels for others.

Through the great popularity of these holy proponents of the prayer wheel practice and the powerful spirit of Tibetans' devotion to Avalokiteshvara, the prayer wheel practice became widespread among the laypeople of Tibet. Today, as one travels among Tibetans in exile in India and Nepal, one inevitably sees many elder Tibetans spinning hand-held mani wheels, or large, stationary mani wheels with visible joy and devotion.

In recent years, the practice of the prayer wheel has gradually spread to the West. Precisely when Westerners first had contact with the prayer wheel lineage is uncertain. Some historians of technology[67] believe that in the fifteenth century, when Catholic prohibitions against taking Christian slaves led Italians to enslave thousands of people from Central Asia, the enslaved may have brought with them some parts of the prayer wheel technology, such as the ball-and-chain governor (from hand-held wheels), the vertical-axis windmill (from wheels turned by wind), and the hot-air turbine (from wheels turned over fireplaces). If this thesis is correct, then one can hardly imagine a more inauspicious beginning for Western contact with this sacred ritual.

In the nineteenth century, Western travelers to Tibet—primarily Christian missionaries—began noting prayer wheels in their writings. There is no term in Tibetan commentaries or in common Tibetan usage that could rightly be translated as "prayer wheel." Christian missionaries appear to have coined the term "prayer wheel" or "praying-wheel." E.R. Huc, an English writer and journalist traveling in Tibet in the mid-1800s, called them "turning prayers," holding that the Tibetans superstitiously believed that the wheels themselves were praying.[68] Tibetans generally use the terms "mani wheel" and "Dharma wheel" when referring to this practice. As the term "prayer wheel" gained common parlance, it lost its original pejorative sense and today is even used by Tibetans in the West. Early misconceptions aside, the term is appropriate. The prayer in this practice is not so much a prayer *to* an external, supernatural being, as it is one of compassion *for* the welfare of others.

Although Mahayana Buddhism has been spreading in the West since the 1950s, the practice of building large and small prayer wheels became popular among Western Buddhists only since the 1990s. With the Tibetan diaspora, Central and East Asian Buddhist practices and art forms have come into increasingly fruitful contact. Furthermore, the integration of modern technology with traditional methods has contributed to innovations in the production of sacred Buddhist art. As a part of this renaissance of Mahayana Buddhist arts and culture, an increasing number of Western artists and artisans have built very beautiful prayer wheels.

Lama Thubten Zopa Rinpoche has been at the forefront of this artistic renaissance. In Bodhgaya, India—the site of the Buddha's enlightenment—he is overseeing the building of a statue of Maitreya, the Buddha of Love, that will dwarf New York's Statue of Liberty. At approximately five hundred feet, it will be the largest metal statue in the world, and it is being engineered to last for over a thousand years. Traditional Tibetan artists and lamas are collaborating with Western artists, East Asian Buddhists, engineers, computer-imaging experts, physicists, and metallurgists to create an artistic expression of enlightened love unique in history. Lama Zopa Rinpoche is also overseeing the building of the largest stupa in the West. Although this stupa is being constructed in Australia using high-tech building methods, its design is based on the structure of the Great Stupa of Gyantse in Tibet, a fifteenth-century masterpiece with seventy-five internal temples. In California, Lama Zopa Rinpoche is overseeing the building of one hundred thousand stupas in a terraced, mandala design based on the famous stupas in Borobudur, Indonesia, the world's largest Buddhist monument (erected circa 780–833). Lama Zopa Rinpoche has also overseen the building of hundreds of smaller stupas and statues, the creation of religious paintings on a scale reminiscent of the Italian Renaissance, and the creation of molds for crafting beautiful, small holy stupas and statues from modern resins and plasters.

In the construction of prayer wheels, Lama Zopa Rinpoche has innovated the use of microfilm technology for printing the mani mantras to be wound inside them. According to tradition, a prayer wheel becomes more powerful with each additional mantra wound inside of it. Thus, by using microfilm, one can build prayer wheels more powerful than any built in Tibet. Lama Zopa Rinpoche has also encouraged the use of modern technology in the design and construction of prayer wheels that last longer and turn more easily. Of course, he insists that the prayer wheels be filled according to instructions in the commentaries and that the outer decorations are made with great care and precision. Similarly, students of Tarthang Tulku have used computerized typesetting equipment to print very small, clear scriptures and mantras to fill beautiful prayer wheels that are turned by electric motors. One such prayer wheel was given to the U.S. Library of Congress and can be seen in the Asian Reading Room.

Through the efforts of Lama Zopa Rinpoche and other lamas and practitioners, prayer wheels continue to be built in Tibetan and other Asian Buddhist communities, as well as in the West. It is my sincere hope that this book may contribute in some way to the flourishing of this lineage of practice, to an ongoing renaissance in Buddhist arts and practices, and to the development of enlightened compassion in the minds of all beings.

✑ PART TWO:

*Tibetan Commentaries
on the Prayer Wheel*

An Oral Discourse

The first commentary in this section is a transcript of an oral discourse on the power and benefits of the prayer wheel, given in June of 1994 by Lama Zopa Rinpoche at the Land of Medicine Buddha in Soquel, California, in dedication of a large prayer wheel built by Jim McCann at Lama Zopa Rinpoche's request. This discourse was transcribed by Jindati Doelter and edited by Briege Wallbridge and Venerable Ailsa Cameron. I have made only minor changes for the sake of consistency with the other translations. With their emphasis on using prayer wheels for healing, Lama Zopa Rinpoche's comments here may be viewed as an experiential and practical commentary on the text translated next in this section. This discourse was originally published in Mandala: Newsmagazine of the FPMT *(Foundation for the Preservation of the Mahayana Tradition). It is reprinted here with the permission of the FPMT and the Wisdom Archive.*

In Solu Kumbu[69] all the old men and women turn a prayer wheel every day. When they are at home in the morning, and in the evening before they go to bed, they hold a mala in their left hand, a prayer wheel in their right, and recite *Om mani padme hum*. And when they walk around, they constantly turn the prayer wheel and recite *Om mani padme hum*. I often used to think: *How does turning the prayer wheel become Dharma practice?* I had this question in my mind simply because I was ignorant as to the benefits of the practice. I didn't know what an important practice it is and how beneficial it is in terms of purification. Just touching and turning a prayer wheel brings incredible purification, and accumulation of unbelievable merit.

At Lawudo I found many old manuscripts, handwritten texts by the Lawudo Lama. The previous Lawudo Lama, who was called Lama [Kunsang] Yeshe—some people think he has something to do with my life—did not have a monastery, but lived in retreat in a cave.[70] He put a lot of effort into copying texts of practices of various Vajrayana deities. At that time such texts were very rare, so he wrote many out by hand. Because they had been stored in the cave, which was very humid, the texts were damp, and I used to dry them in the sun. If you don't dry them, the texts grow fungus and are then destroyed by worms. The worms reincarnate among the texts and make some interesting holes in them!

One day when I was laying the texts out in the sun, I saw one old text with the title *Mani Kabum* [*One Hundred Thousand Mani Teachings*]. It contains all the history of the evolution of the world, including how Dharma came into this world and how the sentient beings of Tibet, the Snow Land, became the particular objects to be subdued by the Compassion Buddha Avalokiteshvara. Amitabha and the Compassion Buddha are the same in essence and are very strongly linked…and, for more than twenty years, the Compassion Buddha and Amitabha have guided Western countries (not only Tibet and China), especially by spreading Dharma.

In *Mani Kabum* I saw a short explanation of the lineage of the prayer wheel practice and a few lines on how to visualize and meditate when you do the practice. In Tibet, and generally wherever there are the Mahayana teachings of Vajrayana, the practice of the prayer wheel has spread. Nagarjuna gave the practice to the lion-faced dakini, who gave it to Padmasambhava, who then brought it to Tibet.

After reading this, I developed faith that the practice was not nonsense, but had valid references and was valuable and meaningful. From this text I got some idea of how powerful the prayer wheel practice is in purifying the mind and in accumulating extensive merits.

In 1987, when I was at Chenrezig Institute in Australia, I noticed that the place had become incredibly peaceful. It felt so serene that you wanted to be there, to live there. Chenrezig Institute had not been like that before, and I wondered why it had changed. At that time, Geshe Lama Konchog was there.

Geshe-la has done a lot of Dharma practice. After he escaped from Tibet, he spent many years in retreat in Milarepa's caves in the Himalayas. He did two thousand *Nyung-nays*, the intensive two-day retreat on the Compassion Buddha that involves taking the eight Mahayana precepts and doing many prostrations and mantras. Geshe Lama Konchog has trained his mind well in the path, so I thought that the serenity of Chenrezig Institute might be due to his bodhichitta.

However, one day near the end of my stay there, the thought came into my mind, *Oh, the change might be due to the prayer wheel—it wasn't here before.* Their prayer wheel is much smaller than the one here at Land of Medicine Buddha, but it also contains many mantras on microfilm and is very nicely made.

Some time later, when I was in Brazil at the invitation of a meditation center there, a student gave me a book written by one of Tarthang Tulku's senior disciples about his experiences when he was in charge of building stupas and prayer wheels in Tarthang Tulku's centers. In one section he mentioned that after a prayer wheel was built, the area was completely transformed, becoming so peaceful, pleasant, and conducive to the mind.

This confirmed my belief, based on my own reasoning, that Chenrezig Institute had become so peaceful because of its new prayer wheel. That somebody else experienced a similar effect from building the prayer wheel helped to stabilize my faith.

There are earth, water, fire, and wind prayer wheels. One of the benefits of the prayer wheel is that it embodies all the actions of the buddhas and bodhisattvas of the ten directions. To benefit sentient beings, the buddhas and bodhisattvas manifest in the prayer wheel to purify all of our negative karmas and obscurations and to cause us to actualize the realizations of the path to enlightenment. All the beings—not only the people but also the insects—in the area where the prayer wheel is built are saved from rebirth in the lower realms; they receive a deva [god] or human body, or are born in a pure land of Buddha.

If you have a mani prayer wheel in your house, your house is the same as the Potala, the pure land of the Compassion Buddha. If you have a prayer wheel next to you when you die, you don't need to *phowa*.[71] Having the prayer wheel itself becomes a method to transfer your consciousness to a pure land. Simply thinking of a prayer wheel helps a dying person to shoot the consciousness up the central channel and out through the crown to reincarnate in the pure land of Amitabha [the Land of Bliss, Skt. *Sukhavati*] or the Compassion Buddha [Skt. *Potala.*].

Simply touching a prayer wheel brings great purification of negative karmas and obscurations. Turning a prayer wheel containing a hundred million *Om mani padme hum* mantras accumulates the same merit as having recited a hundred million *Om mani padme hum* mantras. The prayer wheel here at Land of Medicine Buddha contains 11.8 billion mantras, so turning it one time is the same as having recited that many mantras. In those few seconds, you perform so much powerful purification and accumulate so much merit. Turning the prayer wheel once is the same as having done many years of retreat. This is explained as one of the benefits of prayer wheels.

With the water prayer wheel, the water that touches the wheel becomes blessed. When that water goes into an ocean or lake, it carries the power to purify all the billions of animals and insects there.

I have had a wish, which has recently become stronger, to build a prayer wheel in the ocean. Because I have been requested to help with so many other Dharma projects, the idea of making a water prayer wheel has been postponed. However, when I was in one of the centers in Taiwan recently, in a conversation about prayer wheels, I mentioned the idea. One of the benefactors, who has been running the family business for some years, was very happy to make a water prayer wheel because his father had started the business buying fish. Since the family's prosperity came from fishing, he felt his family owed a lot to the fish, and he already had in mind the idea of doing something to repay or to benefit the fish. When I mentioned the idea of the water prayer wheel, he almost cried, and then he asked, "Why are you telling me to build this prayer wheel?" After I explained the reasons, he was very happy to build a water prayer wheel. I mentioned the idea of building it in the ocean near Taiwan, but he thought to build it in Hawaii, where the water of the Pacific Ocean would touch the prayer wheel and bring great benefit.

A fire prayer wheel is turned by the heat of either a candle or an electric light. The light that comes from the prayer wheel then purifies the negative karmas of the living beings it touches.

It is similar with a prayer wheel turned by wind. The wind that touches the prayer wheel is blessed by the power of the prayer wheel and then has the power to purify the negative karmas and obscurations of any being it touches.

Because prayer wheels are so powerful in purifying negative karmas, I think it is a very good idea to use them. After I explained the benefits of prayer wheels a few years ago at Kopan, Lorne and Theresa voluntarily took it upon themselves to make prayer wheels available to other students who wanted to do the practice. They generously made many small prayer wheels and offered them to many students, including me.

I then offered mine to the king of Nepal. When I mentioned to him that having a prayer wheel helps when one dies, he suddenly became distant. I think it's not a subject commonly talked about with him. He asked, "Do I have to keep this?" So I said, "Yes."

It is also mentioned that prayer wheels stop harms from spirits and other beings and also stop disease, so one idea I have is to use them for healing. Anyone with a disease such as AIDS or cancer, whether or not they have any understanding of Dharma, can use the prayer wheel for meditation and healing. For example, sick people could come to the centers for several hours every day to turn the wheel and do the visualizations.

There are two visualizations. With the first, you visualize light beams coming from the mantras in the prayer wheel, illuminating you and purifying you of all your disease and the causes of disease, your negative thoughts and imprints of these left on your mental continuum. You then visualize the light illuminating all sentient beings and purifying all their sufferings as well as their negative karmas and obscurations.

With the second visualization, beams are emitted from the mantras and, like a vacuum cleaner sucking up dust, they hook all the disease and spirit harms and, most importantly, the cause of disease, the negative karmas and obscurations. All these are absorbed or sucked into the prayer wheel. While reciting five or ten malas of the mantra, you visualize purifying yourself in this way.

At the end, recite some malas while visualizing that the beams emitted from the prayer wheel purify all the sufferings and obscurations of the sentient beings of the six realms. These are absorbed into the prayer wheel and all sentient beings, including you, are then liberated, actualizing the whole path and becoming the Compassion Buddha. You can also do circumambulations with the same visualizations.

If someone with AIDS, cancer, or some other disease meditated like this every day, for as many hours as possible, there would definitely be some effect. I know quite a few people who have completely recovered from terminal cancer through meditation. Even though the person might not know about Dharma, about reincarnation or karma, because they want to have peace of mind now and a peaceful death, because they care about having a healthy body and a healthy mind, they should use this extremely powerful and meaningful method of healing.

I would like to emphasize that every large and small prayer wheel can be used by sick people for healing. This practice is very practical and very meaningful.

Two years ago, I asked Jim McCann to build a prayer wheel here at Land of Medicine Buddha, not only for people to do the practice, but also to bless the land. It helps all the insects and animals as well as the human beings. Jim and his wife, Sandra, put a lot of time and effort into actualizing this extremely beautiful prayer wheel, though I'm sure many other people helped them too. From the depth of my heart I would like to thank them very much for their achievement. A prayer wheel makes the place very holy and precious, like a pure land.

Benefits of the Six-Syllable Prayer Wheel

What follows is the first in a series of translations of Tibetan texts that comment on the practice, benefits, and lineage of the prayer wheel. This first translation is of a text by the Fourth Panchen Lama. An ordained monk, his full name was Losang Palden Tenpay Nyima Chogle Namgyal Pel Zangpo (1781–1852). It was this text that Lama Zopa Rinpoche first told us about at Kopan Monastery in 1991, noting that he was so moved by the explanation of the benefits that he placed the text atop his head and vowed to the Buddha of Compassion that he would spread this practice throughout the world. I first received a copy of a translation of this text from Lama Zopa Rinpoche in 1992. The first half of that translation had been dictated by Lama Zopa Rinpoche to Venerable Frank Brok and Venerable Ailsa Cameron, and the second half had been translated by Samdup Tsering, who was then the translator at Tara Institute, a Buddhist center in Melbourne, Australia. Finally, a number of translators and lamas kindly checked various details of the translation.

This translation has been an impetus and the essential guide for this editor and many others in building prayer wheels of various sizes. The diagrams for building prayer wheels, in the third section of the book, are based on this text.

&Here is an explanation of the infinite benefits received from the practice of the six-syllable prayer wheel of the kind Buddha of Compassion:[72]

Namo Guru Aryalokeshvaraya.[73] Through the force of having trained in the two collections[74] from beginningless time, holy mind filled with the treasure of great compassion, embracing migratory beings in a lasso of light of great affection, Transcendent Compassionate-Eyed One [Avalokiteshvara], guide beings forever!

With faith in the supreme collections of actions of the six syllables, the wish-granting jewel that fulfills every wish, one should accumulate the two collections having jewel origination. Since it is a skillful means of leading beings of supreme, middling, or lesser faculties to high spiritual paths and cessations, I shall here explain the stages of practice of the six-syllable mani wheel, which involve little hardship but have great meaning.

The supreme practice, containing the interpretive and definitive meaning of the heart of the whole teaching integrated into one, is the collected actions of the six syllables. Here, the forms and benefits of this practice will be laid down in a way that is very easy to understand and refers to the explanations of the old scriptures.

The Buddha of Infinite Light [Skt. *Amitabha*] said, "In order to benefit sentient beings of the degenerate age,[75] the benefits of the six syllables are explained here: Anyone who recites the six syllables while at the same time turning the Dharma wheel is equal in fortune to the Thousand Buddhas."[76]

Shakyamuni Buddha[77] said, "Listen well, Dikpa Namsel![78] For the sublime practitioner of the heart meaning [a sublime yogi], turning the inside shaft [of the prayer wheel] once is better than having done retreat for one year. For a middling practitioner of the heart meaning, turning the Dharma wheel once is better than having done retreat for seven years. Even for the lower practitioner of the heart meaning, turning the Dharma wheel once is better than having done retreat for nine years. Turning the Dharma wheel is better than listening, reflecting, and meditating for eons."

Dikpa Namsel then said, "Turning the Dharma wheel once is better than attempting to practice the ten transcendent perfections[79] for a thousand years. It is even better than explaining and listening to the three baskets [Skt. *tripitaka*] and the four tantras for eons."[80]

The savior, Maitreya Buddha, said, "If one offers well divine cloth [decorative scarves or canopies] to the profound Dharma wheel, one will receive excellent clothing for five hundred lifetimes. From the merit of offering the hook,[81] one will proceed along the entire path of liberation. From the merit of having offered the shaft, one will become the guide of all sentient beings.

"One will accumulate more merit than from reciting the secret mantra a billion times. One will be prostrated to by jealous gods [Skt. *asuras*] and harm-givers [Skt. *yakshas*].[82] One will control all three: human beings, wealth, and sustenance. One will become meaningful to behold by anyone with whom one has a connection. Sentient beings who are touched by one's shadow will be liberated from the lower realms.

"In terms of temporary benefits, turning the wheel protects one from all contagious diseases and epidemics. It stops one from choosing bad directions.[83] Contaminations and pollutions from resentments will be overcome.[84] Hosts of demons and interferers will be conquered."

Also, Manjushri[85] said, "One is protected by the Guardians of the Four Directions and the Protectors of the Ten Directions from all the obstacles of the directions and corners. This practice purifies the five uninterrupted karmas[86] and the ten nonvirtuous actions;[87] it purifies all evil-gone actions [causes of rebirth in the lower realms]. One will go to a pure realm of Buddha. One will enter and take birth in the lotus-heart on a lion throne in the Blissful Realm [Sukhavati].[88] One will develop the actions of all the buddhas in the ten directions."

Vajrapani[89] said, "Through this great wheel of Dharma one can stop all those who harm—the demonic planets above, the demonic nagas below, and the hosts of spirits and elementals in between. How can it protect like this? This mantra wheel contains each heart syllable of the five types of victorious ones [Skt. *dhyani buddhas*] such as Buddha Tutob Gyalpo."[90]

Avalokiteshvara said, "This great wheel of the mantra excels other wheels. The fortunate migratory beings who rely upon this Dharma wheel, by turning it and making requests, find the best refuge protector of this and future lives."

The Practice of the Wheel Called Om Mani Padme Hum

The tantra *Unceasing Dharma Wheel* explains: "Make this great wheel extremely carefully without mistakes in the view of the earth and in view of the sky [in view of the earth and sky mantra wheels described below.]" Make the earth, water, fire, and wind Dharma wheels and the compounding hand wheel according to the traditional practice passed through the revealed lineage.

This mani wheel has a head cover [top] and a foot cover [bottom]. The head cover should face the sky; the foot cover, the ground. Those two wheels should be joined and filled, piling up as many as possible according to the size. If one cannot manage to do both, just do as many as possible of the sky wheel or the earth wheel. In fabricating handheld Dharma wheels, there are several types. One is called the "stacked-up" [Tib. *lolangma*]. Others are known as the "male-coiled" [*potrima*] and the "female-coiled" [*motrima*].

The letters of the mantra should face outward; the *Om* should connect to the life-tree or bamboo shaft, and then wind around it. This is the traditional practice of the learned ones. Why is this done? The tantra *Unceasing Dharma Wheel* explains that the syllables of the root mantra should wind around like a snake, with the *Om* connecting to the life-tree and the *Hum* at the end. With the abiding mantra that goes inside statues or stupas, the letters should face inward and be rolled from the end.

Doing it as explained when you are making the Dharma wheels, the tightness of the stacking and winding should be suitable—not too tight and not too loose. If they are too tight, there is the fault like squeezing the mantra between two rocks. If they are too loose, there is the fault like having the intestines loosened [falling out]. One should understand that it has to be done the middle way. No matter what size Dharma wheel one makes, if one of the inserted mantras is wound upside down it is as if all the rest were wound upside down as well. So, when you wind and pile [the mantras], do everything carefully—this is important.

Homage to the Transcendent Compassionate-Eyed One!

The Method for Making the Life-Tree of the Mani

The best material for the life-tree is reddish white sandalwood. The next best is *Acacia catechu*.[91] The last choice is juniper or birch. The life-tree should be very straight and smooth. Not mistaking the top and bottom of the wood's natural growth direction, the top of the letters should face the upper tip of the life-tree's wood.[92]

Then, write *Om*, *Ah*, and *Hum* down the life-tree, dividing the tree into three parts. Below the *Om*, write *Om sarva vidya svaha* as many times as possible. Below this write *Nama samanta buddhya nan, Om vajra ayushe svaha* as many times as possible. Below the *Ah*, write *Om dharmadhatu garbhe svaha, Om sarva tathagata mani shata dam sti jvala jvala dharmadhatu garbhe svaha* as many times as possible. Below the *Hum*, write the mantra of dependent arising—*Om ye dharma hetu prabhava hetun tesham tathagato hyavadat, teshan cha yo nirodha, evam vadi maha shramanah ye svaha*—and *Om supratishta vajra ye svaha* as many times as can fit.[93]

Make the sky wheel with two concentric circles and put a hole in the center through which to fit the life-tree. Outside this [the hole for the life-tree] in the first rim draw a six-petaled lotus. Starting with the eastern petal, write down one syllable of the mani mantra [on each petal], starting with *Om*, with the letters facing out. Outside this are six spokes. On each spoke write *Kam*. Outside that is a rim with six petals. Starting from the east, on the first petal write the six-syllable mani [mantra]; on the second, *Om hum tam hrih ah* [and so on].[94]

Then, the earth wheel is made similarly, but with the letters facing inward. On the first rim, on the inner circle, on the six-petaled lotus, starting from the east, write down one syllable [on each petal], starting with *Om*. On the second rim, write the *Kam* syllables. Then, at the foot of the spokes write the heart of dependent arising mantra, and the mantra *Om supratishta vajra ye svaha*. There are two rims beyond that. On the first one, write the six-syllable mani mantra [all the way around], and on the second write the requesting wishes, at the end of which write *Om shude shude svaha*.

The requesting wish is: "Due to the merits of having built this supreme holy wheel of the supreme speech of the six syllables and turning it, may I and all sentient beings who see, hear, touch, or remember this Dharma wheel be purified in that second of all the negative karmas, obscurations, and negative imprints; be able to achieve the ultimate *dharmakaya*,[95] which is purified of the two obscurations; and be able to lead all sentient beings, who have been our mothers, immediately, in that second, to full enlightenment. May extensive benefits for all sentient beings be accomplished. *Om shude shude svaha.*"

Elaborate Explanation of Benefits

Even though the benefits of making the Dharma wheel have been explained before, here they will be elaborately explained.

Buddha said, "One benefit is that the karma and disturbing thought obscurations that have been accumulated for beginningless rebirths are purified without effort. There is no doubt that it becomes a complete secret mantra, gnostic mantra, and dharani mantra.[96]

The *Tantra of the Unsurpassed Wish-Granting Jewel* says, "By the very turning of this wheel, *Om mani padme hum*, one will be blessed by the gurus, will be granted realizations by the mind-seal deities, will be cared for by the ones gone to bliss [Skt. *sugatas*], and will have obstacles eliminated by the Dharma protectors."[97]

Also, the Transcendent Compassionate-Eyed One left this wheel, which we call *Om mani padme hum*. Each turning of the wheel becomes [the same as having done] the number of [recitations] of the nearing-the-deity retreat.[98] From having written one mantra, [each turn of the wheel multiplies by that] one. Having written ten multiplies by ten; having written one hundred multiplies by one hundred. Ten wheels become thousands, becoming one hundred thousand, and so forth. Since they multiply in this way, the instruction of the practice of the wheel should be cherished.[99]

Not knowing the practice of the Dharma wheel and relying upon other practices is like a blind person trying to see—there is no way to succeed. A person with small wisdom and great laziness is like a donkey sunk in mud. Therefore cherish the practice of the Dharma wheel.

The Visualization of the Wheel
Called Om Mani Padme Hum

The way of visualizing the wheel called *Om mani padme hum* comes in the tantra entitled *The Condensed Secrecy of the Compassionate-Eyed One*. It is as follows: "Light beams from the great Dharma wheel take the delusions, sufferings [Skt. *dukkha*], imprints (or predispositions), and seeds of all sentient beings in the six realms and cause these to be collected and absorbed into the six-syllable wheel. All the disturbing thoughts, karmas, seeds, and imprints are burnt, destroyed, and purified. If one does this practice, one is liberated from the causes, conditions, and results of samsara—from all disturbing thoughts, karma, and obscurations. This is the wheel cutting the root of samsara. Keep extremely secret and cherish this practice.

"Through light beams emanating from the mantras of the precious wheel and striking migratory beings, they spontaneously develop the four immeasurable thoughts—loving-kindness, compassion, joy, and equanimity. They complete the practice of the six perfections—giving, morality, patience, perseverance, concentration, and wisdom."

Vajrasattva[100] said, "By turning this wheel called *Om mani padme hum*, some beings will experience the first ground, extreme joy. From there up to the tenth ground, clouds of Dharma, the ten grounds will be completed. First one completes the five paths, from the path of accumulation up to the path of no more learning, and then one becomes enlightened spontaneously with the resultant five bodies and five wisdoms.[101]

In *Wheel of Wind,* Master Nagarjuna says, "A being who is either touched by the continuum of the wind from the wheel or by the wheel's shadow will be liberated."

Master Padma [Padmasambhava] also says, "The purposes of this wheel are as follows: Even those lacking perseverance in their practice, who pass their time passively, will be able to attain mystic powers by relying on the wheel, while those with perseverance will be helped in verbal recitation. Even enormously sinful actions can be purified effortlessly. By pronouncing and writing [the mantra], one can purify all faults and attain all excellent qualities. By gathering under the shadow of the wheel, migratory beings with the eight fetters[102] can be liberated. By mere contact with the four elements that have activated the wheel, one will be freed from lower rebirths. In short, all unwanted faults can be purified without any effort. Just contacting the wheel once can cause one to achieve liberation and all excellences effortlessly."

Om mani padme hum
Homage to the Great Compassionate One

Origin of the Mani Wheel

The Transcendent Compassionate-Eyed One predicted to Master Nagarjuna, "In the palace of the land of the nagas is the bodhisattva naga king, who is the owner of a profound wheel of Dharma. By hearing, seeing, touching, or thinking of this wheel, one can swiftly attain liberation from the suffering of the three lower rebirths. If you go and fetch this wheel, the benefits to sentient beings will be enormous."

Consequently, Master Nagarjuna visited the land of the nagas and said to the bodhisattva naga king, "O bodhisattva naga king, please pay attention to me. I have come here because the Transcendent Compassionate-Eyed One prophesied that the benefits to sentient beings will be enormous if I beg from you your profound wheel of Dharma, which can liberate beings from all types of sufferings of lower rebirths just by their seeing, hearing, touching, or thinking of it. Kindly give it to me."

The bodhisattva naga king replied, "This wheel of Dharma, which has the quality of quickly liberating all transmigrators from the great suffering of the three lower rebirths merely by hearing, seeing, touching, or thinking of it, was kindly given to us in the past by Buddha Beautiful Lamp [Tib. *Marmezey,*

Skt. *Dipankara*], and it has given the nagas much happiness. Through it, many of them have been led to the grounds and paths of buddhahood. This Dharma wheel is the wheel of the mantra *Om mani padme hum,* the essence mantra of the Transcendent Compassionate-Eyed One received from the buddhas upon request, which represents the essence of all the qualities of the body, speech, mind, and actions of all the buddhas. I shall give this wheel to you. You must place it on or in earth, water, fire, or wind, and you must use it for the sake of Dharma and living beings."

The wheel was passed on to Master Nagarjuna together with its instructions for practice. Master Nagarjuna brought it to India and later passed it on to the angel with the face of a lion. She gave it to the great siddha Tilopa, who gave it to the great scholar Naropa. He gave it to the great translator Marpa who gave it to the lord of yogis, Venerable Milarepa. He gave it to the incomparable Dagpo Lhaje [Gampopa], who passed it on to Khampa U-se [the First Karmapa, Dusum Khyenpa], and it spread pervasively.[103]

Benefits of the Wheel

In the collected writings of Karma Pagshi, an accomplished meditator, many benefits of this wheel are described. Here are some benefits in relation to the practice of placing the wheel on or in earth, water, fire, and wind.

This wheel called *Om mani padme hum,* when blown or moved by the wind above, can release from suffering of lower rebirths those transmigrators who are either touched by the wind's draft or who are dwelling in the wind's direction.

When placed over a fire, it releases from lower rebirths all transmigrators who either smell the smoke or who are illuminated by the light of the fire.

When placed on the earth, it releases from lower rebirths all transmigrators who are living on that earth or who are touched by the earth's particles.

When placed in water, it releases from the suffering of lower rebirths all transmigrators living in the water or who drink it.

Therefore, engage in the practice of the wheel in accordance with the instructions of a qualified master.

If this mani wheel is turned properly, like turning around an umbrella, one will obtain an attractive body with all sense organs intact and perfect. If it is turned around frantically, one will have an inferior body.

If it is turned around on its side, one will be born as an animal with a bowed back. If it is turned upside down, one will be born crippled or without any legs.

If it is not made with clear inscriptions, one will be born blind.

If wrong view is generated toward the sound of the wheel, one will be born deaf.

If one denies the value of the wheel itself [with nihilistic view], one will be born demented [or stupid].

So, if a fortunate person holds this great wheel of Dharma straight and turns it around, one with superior faculties will achieve buddhahood and benefit all transmigrators; one with middling faculties will attain a human life and practice holy Dharma; and even one with lesser faculties will also find a human life and make an effort to abandon nonvirtues and practice virtues.

This wheel of Dharma called *Om mani padme hum*, if constructed inside a house and circumambulated will liberate the family [living in the house] from sufferings of lower rebirths, and the house itself will become like the Potala pure land.[104]

This wheel of Dharma, *Om mani padme hum*, if placed close to a dying person's pillow near the time of death and fervently prayed to from the depths of one's heart, will instantly [cause] one's consciousness to dissolve into the heart of the Transcendent Compassionate-Eyed One without the need for the practice of the transference of consciousness. So, free of doubt, be zealous in constructing this supreme wheel of Dharma and cherish the practice of circumambulating it, and so forth.

To this wheel of Dharma called *Om mani padme hum*, make grand offerings of the various objects of fulfillment such as light, food, and so forth. By making offerings, one will become a universal king and be able to enjoy all one's wishes. Ultimately one will attain the state of the Transcendent Compassionate-Eyed One.

All those with fortune, please show, tell, and spread this wheel of Dharma called *Om mani padme hum* to others. Please spread the benefits of the wheel, for doing so is the same as preserving and spreading the Buddhadharma.

This is an abbreviated explanation of the extensive benefits of the six syllables as explained by the buddhas, bodhisattvas, and learned, highly attained ones [holy beings]. That is all for now.

This has been laid down just in order for the able ones to find faith in the practice, benefits, and origin of making and turning the large mani wheel, the hand mani wheel, and the mani wheels of fire, water, wind, and so forth.

Those of superior intelligence should realize the extensive benefits of the six syllables by listening to, reflecting, and meditating with great zeal on *The Toot Tantra of the Great Compassionate One* and such commentaries as *The Hundred Thousand Mani Teachings* [Tib. *Mani Kabum*], and so forth, which are scriptures that cannot be debated.

Out of non-objectifying compassion, the special deity of Tibet, the Great Compassionate One, who is the nature of all the buddhas' compassion, emitted hundreds of thousands of beams of compassion, making meaningful his being called by the name "Great Compassion." May I and all sentient beings be guided inseparably [by you] until [we achieve] birth in the blissful, pure realms, such as Potala; completion of all the [virtuous] qualities; attainment of the magnificent four bodies [of a buddha] and the heart of enlightenment.

Because of the merits of generating my mind in a pure [mirror-like] form [Skt. *artisha*] as your holy body and reciting the six-syllable mantra, may I purify all negative karmas and obscurations accumulated from beginningless rebirths and become a heroic guide for all beings.

Colophon

Because the ex-abbot of Kumbum, the incarnation of Cheshu Ngawang Shedup Tenpay Nyima, and the ex-doctor Tenzin Gyatso persuaded me that there was a need, I, the virtue-beggar of the Shakya [the monk], Losang Palden Tenpay Nyima Chogle Namgyal Pel Zangpo, have written of the origin of the six-syllable wheel, how to turn it, and the visualization like this, in the bedroom of Kadam Palace. Through this, may all the incarnated beings receive infinite benefit and peace.

Dedication by Lama Zopa Rinpoche

May these merits, if there are any, be the cause for the stable lives of the compassionate ones—His Holiness the Dalai Lama, the virtuous friends, and all holy beings—who have taken human form for the benefit of us sentient beings.

May anyone who hears, sees, touches, or talks about this be able to spread this practice of turning the Dharma wheel to numberless sentient beings, so that they will never be reborn in the three lower realms. May they be liberated from disease, spirit harms, negative karma, and obscurations, generate bodhichitta, and achieve enlightenment. May they then liberate numberless sentient beings.

May mani wheels, particularly those built as a result of this translation, immediately stop all obstacles to the happiness of sentient beings, especially those beings in the immediate area of a mani wheel. May all contagious diseases, wars, famines, and disharmony be eliminated immediately, as well as disease, spirit harms, negative karma, and obscurations. May their minds be completely purified and filled with love and compassion. May their lives be full of the joy of bodhichitta, exchanging self with others. Especially in the immediate area of the wheel, may even the insects be free from and never be reborn again in the three lower realms.

May all wishes be successful according to the Dharma.

May all of us be guided by the Compassionate Buddha and be able to bring temporal and ultimate benefit.

I promise to pray that anyone who has a connection with us be guided by the Transcendent Compassionate-Eyed One in all lifetimes and quickly achieve the Compassionate-Eyed One's enlightenment.

Practice and Benefits of the Prayer Wheel: Having Devotion and Generating Happiness

This next translation is from the collected works of Sengchen Dorje Chang Losang Tenzin Paljor. Born in 1784, Sengchen Dorje Chang was a famous lama of Tashi Lhunpo Monastery—a monastery founded by the First Dalai Lama that, by the late eighteenth century, had become a great center of learning and the seat of the Panchen Lamas. As a tulku, or reincarnate lama, two of his previous incarnations had been abbot of the Tantric College. The Fourth Panchen Lama, who wrote the text translated in the previous section, was one of Sengchen Dorje Chang's personal teachers and thus may have sparked the latter's interest in the prayer wheel. According to the text, the First and Second Panchen Lamas and others had built prayer wheels near Tashi Lhunpo Monastery, and more recently, Sengchen Dorje Chang's teacher, Losang Tenzin Palzangpo, had built a large one.

After Dan Martin brought this text to my attention, I was able to locate a copy through the U.S. Library of Congress. The Venerable Lama Zopa Rinpoche, with the assistance of Venerable Paula Chichester, translated most of the text. Venerable Tsering Tuladhar (Tsen-la), at Lama Zopa Rinpoche's request, translated one section. Venerable Geshe Tsulga and his translator Venerable Damchoe, Wilson Hurley, and Venerable Khenpo Phuntsok Tashi very kindly checked and rechecked difficult passages.

Motivation

&May all who see this text be free of all negative karmas, spirit harms, diseases, afflictions, and the like, and may they be able to practice the mani and actualize the meaning of the mani.

Explanation

Here is the explanation of the practice and benefits of hand-turning the mani [wheel] and so forth, having devotion and generating happiness.[105]

The snow mountain of all the compassion of the victorious ones is melted by the hot beams of the generated holy mind [Skt. *bodhichitta*]. That water becomes a whirlpool that can extinguish the conflagration of the sufferings of transmigrating beings. May that great ocean of compassion be our guide. By saying this, the offerings are expressed. Here I am going to explain a little about the practice and benefits of the mani wheel.

The hand, water, and wind-turning mani [wheels] have spread well throughout Central Tibet, Tsam, Kham, Amdo, and China-Mongolia.[106] A clear explanation of [scriptural] references for these practices doesn't seem to exist in the sutras and tantras of the Qualified Destroyer, the One Gone Beyond [the Lord Buddha]; nor is it found in the scriptural commentaries of the highly attained, great pandits of the noble country of India or of Tibet. It is for this reason that when the omniscient possessor of the victory, Jetsun Losang Jampal Gyatso Pal Zangpo,[107] was asked many questions on the difficult points of sutra and tantra by his own heart son, Kalka Jetsun Dampa Losang Thubten Wangchuk Jigme Gyatso Pal Zangpo, among them was this question: "There is so much [practice of the] hand-turning mani wheel spread in this country, please write down the benefits and send it."

In answer to that, this practice doesn't seem to occur in the traditional practice of Lama Atisha father and son[108] and of Great Tsongkhapa. If, in explaining and clarifying what is to be negated and what is to be accepted, the white crow were difficult to separate from the rest of the crows, I would leave this in equanimity. But it is not. It doesn't seem like turning the mani wheel cannot be done and that it is not of great benefit. At the great monastery of Dharma study, Tashi Lhunpo, on its land below, the great pandit, the omniscient one, Losang Chokyi Gyaltsen and Jetsun Losang Yeshe established so many mani wheels during their time.[109] Even in recent times, in north Reting, Trichen Dorje Chang established a very big mani wheel. And even in this land, our supreme guide, the holy being, great wheel-turner of the highly attained ones, the tutor, Dorje Chang Losang Tenzin Pal Zangpo,[110] established a new, very big prayer wheel, and so forth. If one thinks about these reasons, it is definite that there is something in the mani wheel that has some benefit.

Besides that, the practice of *migtsema*[111] wheel-turning, and so forth, was explained to the highly attained possessor Mingtangpa by Lama Tsongkhapa, in that yogi's pure view.[112] I think it is similar to the practice of the mani wheel. Thus this text has three parts: the evolution of the wheel, the practice of the actual base [how to construct the mani wheel], and the explanation of the benefits.

The Evolution of the Wheel

According to what exists in the stories that have been passed down, when Master Nagarjuna descended to the land of the nagas, he asked the bodhisattva naga king, "Please, naga king, pay attention to me. The Transcendent Compassionate-Eyed One predicted to me, 'You [should] go to the land of the nagas. The bodhisattva naga king has a very profound Dharma wheel. By seeing, hearing, remembering, or touching this Dharma wheel, sentient beings become liberated from all the sufferings of the evil-gone realms.' He asked me to request this wheel [from you] and bring it [back], so I came here. Please compassionately grant this Dharma wheel."

Responding to this request, the bodhisattva naga king [spoke the following words] from his holy mouth, "My profound Dharma wheel, just by being seen, heard, remembered, or touched, quickly liberates the six types of beings from the sufferings of the evil realms. This wheel was given to us nagas by the past Buddha Dipankara. Through it, we nagas became happy, and so many progressed on the path to enlightenment. This Dharma wheel of the mantra *Om mani padme hum* represents the essence of all the qualities of the body, speech, mind, and actions of all the buddhas. Establish it in earth, water, wind, and so forth, and you must use it for the sake of the Dharma and living beings."

The naga king said this and granted the practice. Then Master Nagarjuna brought it to India and gave it to the angel with the face of a lion. She gave it to Tilopa, who gave it to Naropa. He gave it to Marpa, who brought it to Tibet and gave it to Milarepa, who gave it to Dakpo Lhaje [Gampopa], who gave it to U-se Takpa [the First Karmapa, Dusum Khyenpa]. It came down through the lineage to Karma Pagshi.[113] I have seen a handwritten manuscript in the collected works of Karma Pagshi [elaborating] many benefits of the wheel. As Karma Pagshi had high attainments [realizations] and as these references to how the prayer wheel happened appear in his collected works, I think it must be valid, but this is still a point to analyze.

Actual Practices, How to Make the Prayer Wheel[114]

Even though I have seen many different examples of how to do this practice, there is no clear explanation other than that of this learned, highly attained one. So, I'm going to explain here on the basis of that one pure, brief reference:

(1) The life-tree should be [from] a good tree like juniper, sandalwood, and so forth; any of the good trees, but not a poisonous tree. The root and tip of the tree shouldn't be confused. The life-tree should be square or round. On the top, write *Om sarva vidya svaha*. On the side, write the syllables of the holy body, holy speech, and holy mind: *Om Ah Hum*. Then in the middle, *Om vajra ayushe svaha*. Below that, put *Om supratishta vajra ye svaha*, written in full [covering the whole space]. Anoint the tree with sandalwood oil. All the syllables of the mantras should be covered with saffron [the papers with the mantras are painted with saffron water.] It is good if even the ink is mixed with saffron liquid. In regard to rolling the mantras onto the life-tree, whether you start from *Om* or *Hum*, there is no contradiction. At the present time, what is more widespread is rolling the mantra from *Om* with cleanliness.[115] Tie the mantra to the tree well, whether it is the size of a house or small. If you wish, put the sky wheel above [in the top part of the prayer wheel] and the earth wheel below.

How to do the sky wheel: You guess the width of the prayer wheel [and make the diameter of the sky wheel that size]. The center [of the wheel] should be hollow. There are four rims on the inside. If it is elaborate, then five rims. On the first rim draw an eight-spoked wheel and write down *Om mani padme hum hri ah*, starting from the first spoke, clockwise, circling to the right side, starting from the front.[116] On the second rim, write *Om a aa i ii u uu ri rii li lii e ai o au am ah*.[117] Then write this request: "*Svaha*. Please, for the principal benefactor, myself, and all sentient beings, [may we] purify the two defilements, complete the two collections of merit, and quickly achieve full enlightenment. Even for the time being, eliminate all the opposing conditions [obstacles] and actualize all the harmonious conditions exactly according to the wish. *Svaha*." Then on the third rim, write *Om ka kha ga gha nga tsa tsha dza dzha nya ta tha da dha na ta tha da dha na pa pha ba bha ma ya ra la wa shaa sha sa ha ksha hum hum phat svaha*.[118] And, again repeat the request as above. On the fourth rim, write *Om ye dharma hetu prabhava hetun tesham tathagato hyavadat teshan cha yo nirodha evam vadi maha shramanah ye svaha*.[119] On the fifth rim, start from the center [writing]: *Om yamantakrit pragyantakrit padmantakrit bignantakrit achala takkiraja niladanda maha-bala ushnisha chakravarti sumbaraja.* [Also write]: "Please, wrathful control-ling ones, dispel all the harms—black magic, harms by people's talk, and so forth; as well as all the harms done with evil thoughts and violent actions; all harms of spirit possessions, of interferers, of demons, of evil spirits, of the higher and lower intermediate regions[120]—all that can give harm to us, to animals, and to possessions. *Svaha.*" The letters of the upper wheel should be written with the head of the letter facing outward.

On the lower earth wheel, draw the five rims. On the inside one is an eight-petaled lotus. On each petal starting from the front, write down *Om mani padme hum hri ah* as before. On the second rim up to the fourth, start-ing with the front, write down the vowels, consonants, heart of dependent arising mantra, and the requests as before. On the fifth rim, starting from the front, [write]: "*Om Brahma, Indra, Agni, Yama, Dendral* [false spirit], Water God, Wind God, Harm-Giver, Powerful God, Earth Goddess, the Ten Guardians, including their entourages, please protect us, our animals, and all possessions and enjoyments from all opposing conditions [obstacles], and please actualize all harmonious conditions." The letters on the earth wheel are written with the letters facing inward. Behind the back side earth wheel draw a crossed *vajra.* Outside the wheel it should be well covered by paper. Down below, at the lotus and sides, starting from the right side, draw an umbrella, golden fish, wish-fulfilling vase, lotus, conch shell, infinity knot, banner, and *dharmachakra.*[121] Thus it is perfected by virtuous signs. By drawing this, the sky wheel has eight spokes; the earth lotus has eight petals; and, in the mid-dle, the eight auspicious signs make a complete, good collection of virtuous symbols.

The vowels and consonants are the originators of all letters. The heart of the dependent arising mantra is the originator of all blessings; therefore, this has great collections of goodness. Mentioning the names of the wrathful directional guardians and making requests is necessary to protect from obsta-cles the human beings and animals where the prayer wheel is abiding, and to grant realizations. The eight auspicious signs [serve as] the particular offer-ings. Altogether, the purpose is to increase and achieve the auspicious collec-tions of goodness, glorification, and wealth. When these offerings are well done, then wrap the wheel with a white cloth, in accord with the Transcen-dent Compassionate One's holy body. Then cover this layer with a five-col-ored silk cloth. This helps in becoming a dependent arising for one's success in [accomplishing] the four actions. It is said that since the eight auspicious signs are the particular offerings, they should face inside the wheel.

Benefits of the Practice

In accordance with what exists in the teachings of Karma Pagshi, here are the benefits of installing a prayer wheel on earth, water, fire, and wind. When a wind wheel is installed up above, all sentient beings who are touched by this wind or who live in the direction in which the wind [blows] will be liberated from the suffering of the evil-gone realms. When a prayer wheel is installed above a fire, all sentient beings who experience the smell of the fire's smoke or who are struck by the light radiating from this fire will be liberated from the sufferings of the evil-gone realms. When a wheel is installed on the ground, all transmigratory beings touched by the atoms of this earth will be liberated from the sufferings of evil-gone realms.[122] Such and so forth are the benefits.

When a prayer wheel is installed on a high mountain, all the animals living in the mountains and all the sentient beings who are able to see it will be liberated from the sufferings of evil-gone realms. If this great wheel of Dharma, which is a profound Dharma wheel, is placed in a site where many humans and gods visit, all those who frequent this site will be liberated from the sufferings of evil-gone realms.

So forth and so on are the inconceivable benefits. All that is said here is what is said by the Red Buddha. Also, other than this, even though Shakyamuni Buddha, the Great Compassionate One, Dhibsel,[123] and even Maitreya and Manjushri have all spoken extensively, because of many doubts, I didn't write it here. For elaborate, detailed understanding, research the collected works of Karma Pagshi.

Generally, the Supreme, Transcendent, Compassionate-Eyed One is, through karmic fortune, the special deity of the Land of Snows [Tibet]. Even a very sinful person's actions will be purified by recitation and visualization of this six-syllable mantra.

The tantra explaining the mantra of the Great Eleven-Faced, Transcendent, Compassionate-Eyed One states: "Bhagavan-Destroyer, Qualified One Gone Beyond, my essence [the name mantra] is in this way of great magical powers. Recited once, it purifies even the four root downfalls and purifies even the five uninterrupted negative karmas without leaving any single [negative] karma.

"This has been the cause generating the roots of virtue in the many

The main prayer wheel at Kopan Monastery in Kathmandu, Nepal. Depictions of the eight auspicious symbols alternate with the mani mantra written in Landzha script. A canopy hangs above, and sacred paintings cover the walls of the prayer wheel house. [Photo courtesy of Nicholas Dawson]

Additional views of the prayer wheel at Kopan Monastery. A painting of Thousand-arm Avalokiteshvara adorns the wall in the upper right corner. Stylized lotus petals decorate the bottom of the prayer wheel, as shown in the lower photo. [Photos courtesy of Nicholas Dawson]

A prayer wheel in Lhasa, Tibet. Lama Zopa Rinpoche notes that the housing for this prayer wheel is a good model for other prayer wheels. Rinpoche also recommends including a small bell that will ring with each turning of the wheel. [Photo courtesy of Gerry Gomez]

Handheld prayer wheels. *Top:* a woman in Ladakh. *Bottom:* two Tibetan men.
[Photos courtesy of Paul Liebhardt (top) and Kathryn Culley (bottom)]

Rows of prayer wheels built into walls that pilgrims and passers-by can turn as they walk past. In the upper photo, images of the five wisdom buddhas sit above the wheels. In the lower photo, a Tibetan man turns a row of prayer wheels located near the residence of His Holiness the Dalai Lama in Dharamsala, India. [Photos courtesy of Kathryn Culley (top) and Paul Liebhardt (bottom)]

Elaborately decorated
prayer wheels.
Top: Chenrezig Institute,
Queensland, Australia.
Bottom: Nepal
[Photos by Venerable
Roger Kunsang]

An ornately painted prayer wheel at Trakshindo Gompa in Solo Kumbu, Nepal. Below the mantras are paintings of offering goddesses and auspicious symbols. One can also see buddha images painted on the walls around the prayer wheel.
[Photo courtesy of Joseph Sieck]

A large prayer wheel in the new Tibetan Buddhist medical center in Thimpu, Bhutan.
[Photo courtesy of Christina Wood Baker]

Lama Zopa Rinpoche's prayer wheel catches the sunlight in Taos, New Mexico.
[Photo courtesy of Venerable Roger Kunsang]

hundreds of thousands of millions of tens of millions of thousands of millions of buddhas. So, there's no need to say that if you do the recitation and practice, it completely fulfills all their wishes.

"Whoever on account of me does the abiding in retreat [*Nyung-nay* retreat][124] on the fourteenth and fifteenth [of the lunar calendar] will have cyclic existence reduced by forty thousand eons. Bhagavan-Destroyer, Qualified One Gone Beyond, those that hold my name have meaning more extraordinary than the buddhas.

"All the sentient beings who hold my name will come to abide in the state of a non-returner. They will be completely free from all the experiences of sicknesses. They will be completely free from all the obscurations and from harmful actions of body, speech, and mind. Why is this so? Because if any one does the practice exactly according to the method, it is stated that one can attain the enlightened state of a buddha.

"Also, negative karmas, such as that of stealing from the sangha, that cannot be purified by other means, can be purified by this method.

"From the mantra of the fully completed, extensive mind of Great Compassion, it is stated that any sentient beings who have created negative actions of misusing and wasting food and other material possessions belonging to the sangha community cannot be purified even if they declare and confess with regret in the presence of the thousand buddhas who came to this world. However, by reciting this mantra of great compassion, all those will be purified. The negative action of misusing and wasting food and other material possessions belonging to the Triple Gem can be purified eventually, if declared and confessed before the eyes of the buddhas of the ten directions who are directly perceived. While reciting the mantra of the Great Compassionate One, the buddhas of the ten directions will come there and give empowerments and purify all the negativities and obstructions. All negative karmas, such as the ten nonvirtues, the five uninterrupted negative karmas, disparaging the buddhas, disparaging the Dharma, destroying a confession ceremony, destroying ethics, destroying a stupa, destroying a monastery, stealing material things belonging to the sangha, causing transgressions in those who are living by completely pure moral conduct, and all other extremely negative karmas are completely purified." This is how it is stated.

At the break of dawn, recite the prayers or praise like the *Potoe* (from the *Nyung-nay*) taught by Gelongma Palmo.[125] Even [recite] the short prayer of praise:

Your white, holy body is unstained by faults,
Your head is adorned by a fully completed buddha,
Seeing transmigratory beings with eyes of great compassion.
I prostrate to you, Avalokiteshvara.

This is a prayer composed by Gelongma Palmo herself as the abbreviated meaning of the longer prayer of praise called *Potoe*. Even if one knows only this prayer of praise, if one does it with faith and belief, making the requests, remembering the six-syllable mantra, and turning the prayer wheel, then even those with the dullest of minds, with the heaviest of negative karmas, of the lowest of castes, be they however inferior, regardless of whether they are men or women, because the Transcendent One's compassion is without bias of feeling close to some or distant from others, all are liberated from sicknesses, epidemics, harm of spirit possessions, and all obstacles. All their mistaken thoughts and wrong views cease, and they are able to proceed to happiness. All the realizations of the path are increased higher and higher. All the necessities of this world and beyond this world are fulfilled.

These statements pledged by honorable words of truth are for us to generate trust and to have faith and belief and thereby make single-pointed requests. One never needs to doubt their benefits.

All these latter benefits were stated by the highly learned and powerfully accomplished Je Gungtang Konchog Tenpe Dronme as part of the ornamental teachings on the *Nyung-nay*. Because of the excellence of this advice, it has been incorporated here as well.

Generally, for whatever Dharma one is accomplishing, first begin with a pure motivation of bodhichitta. The practice should be pure without additions and omissions and without mistakes. The end should be concluded with pure prayers of dedication for the fully completed state of enlightenment and for the increase in the spread of the teachings. By adorning the dedication with the view of emptiness of the three spheres, one makes the great completion of all the noble conduct of the bodhisattvas without anything missing. So, therefore, dedicate with perseverance.

With this ship of holding your holy name, may we cross the monstrous ocean of suffering in the evil-gone realms to the island of goodness of higher rebirth and liberation. There is no one but you, supreme deity, giving the breath of happiness. Your divine action is the practice of the prayer wheel. By the white virtues of explaining briefly the benefits of it, may all transmigratory beings become inseparable from the supreme guru and may we quickly attain the state of the Transcendent One.

Benefits of the Lotus Wheel

This next translation is based on the longest Tibetan text located regarding the practice of the prayer wheel. The text was located with the assistance of Dan Martin. The author gives his name at the end of the text as Rinchen Nampar Gyalwa. Lama Zopa Rinpoche believes the author was a lama of the Nyingma tradition of Tibetan Buddhism. Lori Cayton and Khamlung Tulku translated the text in full. To reduce repetition, I have deleted long sections that also appear in the Fourth Panchen Lama's text. Some other sections were checked against third sources and edited for consistency of meaning. Existing translations of the two other texts that appear in their entirety in this text were compared against the current translation and resulted in changes of some difficult passages. Many passages that appear in verse in the Tibetan are here translated as prose. These changes were made for clarity; the editor takes responsibility for any errors.

&℘ In the Indian language [the title of this text is]: *Vritachakragatha;* in the Tibetan language [it is]: *Pekhorgyi Penyon Tsigsu Chepa* [*Expressing the Benefits of the Lotus Wheel in Verse.*]

I make salutations to the Three Precious Ones—the excellent ones possessing wisdom [who reside] in the world to turn the wheel of Dharma. The great wise one, Shariputra, asked the Teacher, "By turning the lotus wheel, how can one become fully ripened?" [Thus] he asked the Excellent Most Fortunate One of the World, the Complete Guide. [In response] to that, the Teacher replied:

"I will briefly touch upon the benefits of turning the lotus wheel. For those who turn the lotus wheel [which is adorned with] cloth during the times of the great festivals, and also daily, it is like the continuous flow of an unobstructed river. For those sentient beings in the three [lower] realms [the turning] churns them up from the depths [of the lower realms]. Holding [the lotus wheel] with their hands and seeing it with their eyes will close the doors to evil rebirths. Also, the beings of places such as the sun, the moon, rivers, earth, stones, and orchard groves who turn the wheel with their hands, wherever they are in the six realms, will obtain buddhahood. If one turns [the lotus wheel] on the top of the great mountain [Mount Meru], auspicious qualities will arise in all the realms.

"If a yogic practitioner turns [the lotus wheel], the two aims will be spontaneously accomplished. If a monk turns [the lotus wheel], all the broken vows will be renewed. If a tantric practitioner turns the [lotus wheel], the defilements will be purified and the face of the deity will appear. If a healer [turns the lotus wheel], all illnesses will be cured and buddhahood will be attained. If a king turns [the lotus wheel], the defilements of [his] subjects will be purified. If a minister turns [the lotus wheel], the virtues will increase, reversing the effect of defilements. If a queen turns [the lotus wheel], defilements will be purified, completing the accumulation of merit, and her kingdom will flourish. If a general turns [the lotus wheel], the defilements accumulated [from fighting] enemy armies will be purified. If a soldier turns [the lotus wheel], his own life will be protected, and he will cleanse the obscurations. If a merchant turns [the lotus wheel], the defilements of [doing] business will be purified, all wishes will be achieved. If laypeople turn [the lotus wheel], they will attain the higher rebirths of the gods. If a woman turns [the lotus wheel], she will obtain the pure, precious male body.[126] If a beggar turns [the lotus wheel], the [seeds of previous deeds] of charity will be revived and their own defilements will be cleansed. If the lotus wheel is turned for one day, [the effects] become like millions [of recitations]. Thus it has been taught by the unexcelled *tathagatas*.

"The reciting of the mantras, turning by hand, and visualizing the object of the mind—one should not separate from these three [but] voluntarily take them on. If one wants to practice that holy Dharma [that is, reciting mantras, turning the wheel by hand, and visualizing], the excellent instructions that lead to the next life, one should do just like that. If one wants to purify the defilements, one should do just like that. If one wishes for liberation from the eighteen realms of the hells, one should do just like that. If one wishes for buddhahood in the excellent pure lands, one should do just like that.

"With respect to the teachings on the five ways of turning the wheel, it is explained that there are five [types of wheels]—the fire wheel, the wind wheel, the water wheel, the ground wheel, and the hand wheel. If the wheel is turned in fire, wherever the smoke [of that fire] pervades, all the sentient beings will [attain] buddhahood. If the wheel is turned in wind, wherever that wind blows, all sentient beings will [attain] buddhahood. If the wheel is turned by water, wherever that water flows, all the sentient beings will [attain] buddhahood. If the wheel is turned on the ground, all sentient beings who dwell in that place will [attain] buddhahood. If the wheel is turned in the hand, whomever sees, hears, recalls, or touches that person who is turning [the wheel] will [attain] buddhahood without taking a long time. Even though there are immeasurable merits in [doing actions] such as these, this concludes the brief arrangement [with regard to the five types of wheels].

"*Aryalokiteshvarayah.* The way to turn the mani wheel of the Great Transcendent Compassionate-Eyed One is explained [as follows]: The earth, water, fire, wind wheels, or the hand wheels may be all turned, and so forth. The top and bottom [of the mantra on the mani wheel] should be a continuous link without flaw; it should be written without mistakes, not leaving out or adding anything, and with such [materials] as gold, silver, the special vermilion ink, or with whatever can be found.

"For the life-tree [of the mani wheel], it is good to use iron. For the top and bottom [of the rod] sandalwood is used. The cloth is rolled around without mistaking top for bottom [and vice versa].

"The benefits of turning [the mani wheel] one time will instantly exhaust the karmic defilements [Skt. *klesha*], the obstacles [to nirvana], and the instincts accumulated since beginningless time. It is said that by turning the [mani] wheel, one will achieve all the excellent necessities without even doing as one's main recitation the secret mantras, mantras of the family [that is, the *dhyani buddha* family], or the hidden mantras."[127]

In the *Latticed Lotus Tantra* it says, "The benefits of turning this wheel once with single-pointed concentration are [like a] light illuminating the path. The light rays emanate from the mantras [inside the wheel] and then touch sentient beings, [causing them to] generate [within] themselves the four immeasurable [thoughts] of love, compassion, joy, and equanimity, and then complete the six perfections—giving and the rest. After they attain [realizations] from the [first ground], extreme joy, up to the tenth [ground], clouds of Dharma, completing the five paths and ten grounds, they will obtain the resultant three bodies, the five wisdoms, and simultaneously arisen buddhahood."

In *Presentation of the Wheel* by Padmasambhava, it says, "Those beings who have heard the sounds of the wheel turning, have been touched by its shadow, and have washed or drunk the water blessed by it, will suddenly reduce to a trickle their moral downfalls."

In the *Lotus Garland* the Victorious One said, "The purpose of this wheel is for [the benefit of] those individuals who are in a situation in which they lack diligence. [If they] cherish greatly the instructions about the wheel, they will come to possess diligence. By reciting the mantras and turning the wheel, without a doubt they will obtain the ten grounds [of the bodhisattvas]. Also, for those who possess immeasurable nonvirtues and defilements, [these] will be instantaneously exhausted. Also, whether one wants to obtain the [state of the] meditational deity or of the desire-realm gods, by means of this alone they will be obtained. Even without the intent [to extinguish one's faults and the like], should one be made by someone else to write [mantras] or turn [the wheel], the faults will be exhausted and the positive qualities completed. As for those beings in impure lower realms, they will be liberated from the lower realms by merely being touched by the breeze from a wind-turned wheel or the like."

In short, by merely touching, seeing, or hearing [the wheel], one will become liberated without any effort from the mass of immorality, such as the [negativity] of breaking the root and secondary vows of the monks and nuns, etc. Having extracted quotes from the various tantric texts on the benefits of the individual instructions and arranged them well, these are the poetic verses on the holy wheel.

May those human beings that have manifested the three practices [taking the *kayas* as the path] be introduced directly to the three intermediate states. [And] may they realize the three selflessnesses.

In *Turning the Great River Sutra*, it says, "Make the root wood [the handle or base] from the wood of the bodhi tree and bodhichitta will naturally be generated. The solid central rod should be made from iron and the lifespan of the yogis will be firm and steady. The *Mani hum* being toward the root, and *Om* being rolled on the outside with the various cloths—then merits, possessions, and wealth will increase. The turning of the ornament on the top symbolizes the infinite appearance of the truth body [Skt. *dharmakaya*] and the continuity of the truth body working for the benefit of sentient beings. The turning of the middle of the wheel symbolizes the great compassion of the enjoyment body [Skt. *sambhogakaya*] and the continuity of perfecting the pair of the two truths. Then, the encircling valance is the emanation body [Skt. *nirmanakaya*] continuously working for sentient beings.[128] The conch, attached so that the stone turns [the wheel], is the continuity of the generation of virtuous actions by the disciples. The encircling umbrella at the top [of the mani wheel] is— after one completes all the [five] paths and [ten] grounds—the continuity of the perfection of the abandonments, realizations, and emptiness."

In the *Dredging the Depths of Samsara Tantra* it says, "[Regarding] the person who turns this precious wheel, whatever beings this person sees, hears, remembers, or touches will obtain total completion [of merits], cleanse all the defilements, and obtain buddhahood."

In the *Embodiment of Realization of the Victorious One*, it says, "The Victor said, 'Turn the mantra wheel with water, wind, or the hand while reciting [the mantra] and making offerings.' One profits by simultaneously repeating recitations and turning [the wheel]. One purifies by reciting the mantras and also by turning [the wheel]. In this life, for the purpose of [attaining] buddhahood, diligently turn [the wheel].

"When the wheel is turned with water, the sentient beings that live in the water and the sentient beings that drink that water will complete the [accumulation of] merits, purify defilements, and obtain enlightenment. When the wheel is turned by fire, whatever nonvirtues done by those in the home [will be purified] and the sentient beings touched by the smoke will complete the [accumulation of] merits, purify defilements, and obtain enlightenment. Thus it has been said. When the wheel is turned by the wind, the sentient beings that are touched by that wind will complete the [accumulation of] merits, purify defilements, and obtain enlightenment. Thus it has been said."

With regard to the visualizations of turning the wheel, for the practice of the wheel of the Compassion Buddha:

> When continuously turning the wheel,
> You can see the wheel turning like clouds in space.
> Avalokiteshvara's kindness is like lightning descending from the sky.
> Blessings fall like rain to the earth.
> The disciple ripens like a good harvest.

Such images may come into your visualizations and your dreams."[129]

The eighth instruction on the mani wheel was given to the lion-faced angel by the male and female consorts of the five buddha families. The lion-faced one considered who would be a suitable vessel to be given this wheel of hers. She roamed through India, China, Nepal, Khotan [Tib. *li*], Kabul [Tib. *Orgyen*], Persia [Tib. *Tagzig*], Sri Lanka, and Tibet. She saw that the suitable vessel was the glorious protector, Transcendent Nagarjuna, and she gave it to him. Nagarjuna practiced this single-pointedly. During that time, he put many wheels on top of his meditation hut that were turned by the wind. Because of doing this practice, he saw many manifestations of his meditational deity, the Compassionate-Eyed One, appearing clearly like stars in the sky. After that, unthinkable knowledge was born in his mind. Nagarjuna asked his benefactor, a Dharma king, to make a wheel containing the canon of Buddha's teachings to be turned. And then later, the great Marpa the Translator, checked [these instructions]. Even now, the turning of the Dharma wheel is practiced. Thus it is said.[130]

Nyagtrug Jangchub Senge said, "If one turns the wheel once, the benefits are equal to reading the canon of Buddhist commentaries [Tib. *Tengyur*] once. If one turns the wheel twice, the benefits are equal to reading all the teachings of the Victorious One. If one turns the wheel three times, the defilements of body, speech, and mind are purified. If one turns the wheel ten times, the defilements, even as much as Mount Meru, are purified. If one turns the wheel a hundred times, one becomes equal with the Lord of Death himself. If one turns the wheel a thousand times, the meaning of the truth body of self and others is realized. If one turns the wheel ten thousand times, the purposes of other sentient beings and oneself are fulfilled. If one turns the wheel a hundred thousand times, one will be born within the circle of the Buddha of Compassion. If one turns the wheel one million times, the six types of sentient beings will obtain the great ocean of bliss. If one turns the wheel ten million times, one will be lifted out of the samsaric pit—the abode of the hells. If one turns the wheel one hundred million times, one will become equal to the Transcendent Compassionate-Eyed One."

A few of the wisdom expressions will now be explained, although there are many systems that are explained in the sutras and tantras. In *The Great River Sutra*, Shakyamuni said, "Listen well, Dikpa Namsel! The benefit of turning the Dharma wheel once is greater than the excellent yogis' meditating seven times on the essential meaning. Also, the benefit of turning the Dharma wheel once is greater than exerting effort for eons on the practice of the six perfections. The benefit of turning the Dharma wheel once is greater than teaching or listening for eons to the three baskets and the four classes of tantra. If one does the practice, that is, reciting the six syllables and simultaneously turning the Dharma wheel, one will have [good] fortune with a thousand buddhas. If one offers cloth to the Dharma wheel, for the next five hundred lives one will continuously have comfortable clothes, hats, shoes, and the like. By the merit of offering the [central] iron rod, one will progress along the swift path to the higher state of nirvana. The merit of offering the paper [for the mantras inside] is said to be superior to the merit of reciting a hundred thousand million secret mantras. The merit of offering the wheel's stone-weight [for turning the wheel] is equal to doing immeasurable numbers of recitations. Through the merit of offering the golden top-knob, for eons one will have a perfectly complete accumulation of wealth and possessions. By the merit of offering homage [to the wheel], one will possess a good family and an intelligent, clear mind.

"The individual who turns the Dharma wheel will become the child of a thousand buddhas and will become the guardian of all the transmigrators. [That individual] will make millions of offerings of gods and humans. [That individual] will have control over the three—humans, wealth, and food.

"The temporary great benefits of turning the wheel are: One is relieved of all headaches and plagues; all evil spirits and evil antagonisms are expelled; also, contaminants from pollution are destroyed; the forces of evil spirits and interferers are destroyed; the four [directional] kings and the ten directional guardians will protect [one] in the [four cardinal] directions and the [intermediary] directions. Because of that, the benefits [of turning the wheel] are inconceivable.

"'The ultimate great benefits of turning the wheel are that it purifies the five uninterrupted karmas, the ten nonvirtuous actions, and all evil-gone actions [causes of rebirth in lower realms]. One will go from buddha-field to [buddha-]field. As soon as one is born into the heart of the lotus in the pure land, the actions of all the buddhas in the ten directions will be extended throughout the ten directions.' It is quoted like that by one of the eight bodhisattvas.

"If the [wheel] is placed up high in the wind, whoever is touched by the wind [that turns that wheel] is drawn out from the lower rebirths. If the [wheel] is placed lower by a fire, whoever is touched by the smoke [that turns the wheel] is drawn out from the lower rebirths. If the [wheel] is turned by water, those sentient beings who drink, touch, or dwell in that water will be born in the pure lands. If this water evaporates and reaches the clouds, then the rain from the clouds will lead all the sentient beings [it touches] from the lower realms. Whenever one does the practice of turning the mani wheel by hand, without a doubt one will become enlightened.

"If the [wheel] is placed on the crown of the head at the time of death, then there is no need for transference [Tib. *phowa*]. If one has a mani wheel [and] turns it, one will have a sound body with all [five] sense organs complete. If one turns the mani wheel too rapidly, one will be born mentally disturbed. If one turns the mani wheel sideways, one will be born stooped over. If [the mani wheel] is upside down, one will be born physically handicapped.

"If one meets a person who is carrying the wheel in his or her hand, even a sentient being who has killed his or her own parents will be free from lower rebirths. Also, the sentient beings who see someone turning the wheel on top of a bridge will be free from lower rebirths. If the mani wheel is set up inside a home, that home will become a celestial abode. All those who have seen, heard, been attracted to, had faith toward, remembered, and have touched a mani wheel with their hand, after being liberated from the lower rebirths, will without a doubt be born into the realms of the pure lands." These expressions showing the sources and benefits of the mani wheel are within the text, *Pleasurable Speech Beyond Death*.

Homage to the Transcendent One of Great Compassion. This country, Tibet, has been looked after by the Transcendent Compassionate-Eyed One. Because of that blessing, it is natural for everyone, from young children on up to [adult] men and women, including the ordained, to know the sound of *mani*. The more popular *sadhanas* [methods of attainment] of that [Compassion Buddha], that is, all the profound sadhanas combined, are primarily about the well-known *Teachings of the King* [Tib. *Gyalpo Kabum*] [from] the accomplished Ngodrub. The cycle of oral transmissions, *Disclosure of the Hidden*, and the like [were clearly revealed by] Nyang. From the great histories, which are a part of the Dharma cycles, and which were compiled into one, such as the [concealed] treasures of Tenpa, etc., it says, "the self-arisen body, the self-arisen speech, the self-arisen mind." With regard to the self-arisen speech, it is prophesied by the completely perfect Buddha, "[After] not seeing me from now until one hundred twelve years [from now], there will be a fully ordained monk named Naga. That [monk] will clarify my teachings."

This scholar, Nagarjuna, checked with his clairvoyance if there was an individual who would be a suitable follower of the Great Compassionate One [and who] would benefit all others. After examining, he saw that a young person who was herding buffalo appeared to be the fortunate one. Then, he asked the young buffalo herder, "Do you always herd buffalo?"

Having been asked, the young one said, "Not all the time. I [also] do Dharma practice."

"Then I will teach you."

The young one requested, "If you give me the Dharma, may I accept well the visualization of one deity, and may I accept the recitation of one essence [mantra]."

From the mouth of the scholar [Nagarjuna], "What is it that comes in your mind and in your dreams?"

With regard to that the boy said, "Only the buffalo calves."

To that the scholar said to the young one, "Meditate on the buffalo calves and the Great Compassionate One, and then recite *Om mani padme hum*. From the heart of the Great Compassionate One, light is emitted that dissolves into oneself. One's own heart [also] emits light that reaches the Great Compassionate One. Visualize all appearances as the Great Compassionate One." Because of that [advice], the young one did visualizations and recitations every day. At night [the young herder] cut the grass and put a pair of bundles onto the buffalo, and while coming home the next year at that same time, from the heart of the buffalo there appeared a sack. From that [sack], there emerged an infant child [holding] in his hand a golden rod with *Om mani padme hum* embossed in pearls. [The infant] put the rod into the hand of the buffalo herder. He initiated and blessed [the herder]. The [herder] prostrated to and circumambulated the infant, and then asked for oral teachings.

[The infant replied]: "You should know in your own mind that the Great Compassionate One is the meditational deity. You should know that that mind is clear and empty. You should know that that emptiness is the truth body and unproduced. You should know that the clarified essence is the natural sound of reality itself." Having recited such admonishments, the deity disappeared into space just like a rainbow.

Each evening the herder passed by, herding the buffalo. Then, one time the local people saw circles of light being emitted from [the form] of the Great Compassionate One. They then received him, made prostrations, and scattered flowers. After they did that, the herder spoke. "What are you mistaking me for? I am only a buffalo herder," he said. Then the people said, "You appeared as the Great Compassionate One. You are the object of our prostrations, and the object of our offerings." Having said that, they accepted him as their object of offering. With that, the buffalo herder's body changed, leaving no trace [of its previous form], and went to the pure land of the *dakinis*. Each day, the human beings of this world generate the desire for the exclusive and the common attainments. Thus it is quoted [in the histories of Nagarjuna].

The sentient beings who have not purified their [negative] karma do not see [the Great Compassionate One]. It is said that the [golden] rod that has the self-arisen essence [of *Om mani padme hum*] still exists in Nagarjuna's monastery, Sergyi Jakang. [Nagarjuna] is the scholar of the temple that is northwest of Patna.

[*The next section of this translation is identical to the section of the text by the Fourth Panchen Lama—Losang Palden Tenpay Nyima Chogle Namgyal Pel Zanpgo—which describes Nagarjuna's journey to the land of the nagas to receive the prayer wheel from their king. Following this, a few quotations on the benefits of the prayer wheel also repeat sections of that text. Therefore, these materials are not included here.*]

"If this great Dharma wheel is put on a high mountain, then those sentient beings who abide on that mountain and the transmigrators who move up to the higher realms, all of them will be liberated from the sufferings of the lower realms. If [the wheel] is put on a road in a valley, then those who travel on that road will be liberated from the sufferings of the lower realms. [That road] becomes like the steady path to enlightenment. If [the wheel] is put on a bridge, then those who travel on that bridge will be liberated from the sufferings of the lower realms. [That bridge] becomes the great bridge of Dharma.

"If the profound Dharma wheel is put in the gathering places of the communities of gods and humans, then those who travel through those places will be liberated from the sufferings of the lower realms. [Those gathering places] will become great places of Dharma. If one meets [the Dharma wheel] on the road for the first time, those transmigrators who meet [the Dharma wheel] in that way will be liberated from the sufferings of the lower realms and they will meet the Compassionate-Eyed One. If one stays at home and turns the wheel, then all those transmigrators who abide in that home will be liberated from the sufferings of the lower realms, and their residence will become the Potala [the abode of the Compassion Buddha].

"When placing [the wheel] on the pillow at the time of death, if one focuses the mind and makes supplications, then one will not need to have transference [of consciousness] and the like done. One's consciousness will, in one second, be transferred to the heart of the Compassionate-Eyed One. One should act without having second thoughts or doubts about the profound great Dharma wheel. [One should make] great efforts in raising Dharma wheel[s], establish powerful intent to turn [the wheel], and cultivate great diligence in engaging [in the practice]." Thus it is said.

[The next few paragraphs of this translation are again identical to quotations from the Fourth Panchen Lama's text and are therefore not included here.]

...[Through] the merit of offering precious jewels [to the Dharma wheel], one will have perfect possessions for eons.

Also, in other [texts] it says, "If one offers the [various] types of jewels such as gold, silver, turquoise, coral, pearls, and the like to this great wheel called *Om mani padme hum*, one will enjoy a mass of precious treasures and continuously be endowed with precious ornaments. If one offers inner coverings [of materials] such as brocade, cotton, woolen cloth, and the like, one will enjoy thin, soft brocades for garments and one will [also] enjoy the *pañcalika* clothes [a thin, soft cloth worn by the gods]. If one offers the outer covers such as [those of] brass, copper, leather, and the like, one will enjoy the mesh armor of heroes and one will be endowed with the *vajra* rock of longevity. If one offers a fan, one's luck will be increased, and one will accomplish all the hidden mantras of the essential Dharma. If one offers the golden knob, one will be bound to a high caste and endowed for eons with doing Dharma practice and the good qualities of insight and understanding. If one offers the stone that turns [the wheel], it will be similar to turning the hidden mantras of the essential Dharma, and one will possess the turning of the Dharma wheel. If one offers garlands of wheels, then whoever has contact with the wheels will have happiness and all their acquaintances and friends will benefit. If one offers the iron hook, all the sentient beings will be led by the hook of compassion and also oneself will be led by the hook of compassion. If one offers iron, every era of weapons will decline and afterward no longer arise, and also oneself will be liberated from the era of weapons. If one offers wood, all the sentient beings will possess the bodhi tree, and also oneself will possess bodhichitta. If one offers the various offering objects, such as various necessities—butter lamp, food, and so forth—one will become a wheel-turning king, enjoy whatever one wants, and finally attain the state of the Transcendent Compassionate-Eyed One. If fortunate beings show this mani wheel to others and propagate the teachings of the wheel, it is like protecting and propagating the teachings of the Buddha."

Concerning the visualization of the wheel called *Om mani padme hum*, [it says in] *The Condensed Secrecy of the Compassionate-Eyed One* [Skt. *Avalokiteshvara Guhyasamaja Tantra*]: "Light beams emanating from the great Dharma wheel dissolve the disturbing thoughts, karma, and sufferings of all sentient beings and the instinctual seeds for the six realms into the six-syllable wheel. One thinks that the disturbing thoughts, karma, and seeds, and the instinctual seeds for the six realms are destroyed absolutely and purified. If one possesses this instructional advice, then one will be freed without exception from all the causes, conditions, and results of samsara and from one's disturbing thoughts, karma, and all the negativities and obstructions.

"The wheel is what cuts the root of samsara. One practices with extreme secrecy. Light rays will emanate from the mantra of the precious wheel in motion and then reach the living beings who will instantaneously realize the four immeasurables of love, compassion, joy, and equanimity. They will complete the six perfections of generosity, morality, patience, joyous effort, concentration, and wisdom."

And it is explained that, "Also, when reciting the mantra *Om mani padme hum*, the sound of each syllable is like a bees' nest being destroyed, making the sound 'dirdirrrr.' Not only that, [but] externally [each syllable] is the natural sound of the [specific] elements, and internally the sound is of the sentient beings of the six realms who transmigrate, and so on. Realizing that all those sounds are, themselves, the sounds of the six syllables, if one recites with a mind not wandering onto other things, single-pointedly, with faith and intention, then immeasurable benefits, such as quickly obtaining realizations and the like, will occur."

Again, from the mouth of a Transcendent One, it says, "Even with each turning of the wheel, one [turn] is multiplied by two, ten [turns] are multiplied by ten, eighty thousand [turns] are multiplied by one million, and a hundred thousand, etc. are multiplied a thousand times. And, because of that, one should cherish the instructional advice for the wheel." Since it is also said [like that], it is the inconceivable weapon.

In regard to the things mentioned above, I've just told what I have heard [about] questions asked previously. My own intelligence is limited and I have not experienced great insights with regard to these matters. Because of that, I do not have the courage to present with much pride reasons [that may lead] to genuine certainty; [yet] these instructions cannot be ignored. Please do not be embarrassed by my insisting on explaining [this topic and] allowing the sphere of Dharma [to be explained by me].

[This was written] by Rinchen Nampar Gyalwa in response to the inquiry of Tedai Chingwadur.

A Short Treatise on Prayer Wheels

The following is a translation of a commentary on the prayer wheel written by the famous lama Gungtangpa (1762–1823). His full name was Gungtang Konchog Tenpe Dronme. The text was written at the request of "a monk in the largest Mongolian monastery," located in Urga, the capital, today known as Ulan Bator. Gungtangpa focuses on the symbolism of the prayer wheel and also briefly mentions the visualizations and benefits. This commentary differs from the previous ones in several ways. Gungtangpa does not focus primarily on prayer wheels filled with the mani mantra. At one point, he says "whatever sutra or mantra may be enclosed." Also, he was apparently unfamiliar with the story of Nagarjuna's obtaining the prayer wheel from the nagas. Still, his descriptions of the origins and underlying symbolism of the prayer wheel are interesting. This translation by Dan Martin first appeared in The Journal of the Tibet Society (Vol. 7), *Bloomington, Indiana, 1987, and is reprinted here with the translator's permission.*

☙Homage to Buddha, Dharma, and Sangha.

To speak briefly on the origin of prayer wheels, their accompanying contemplative visualizations, and the benefits of using them, and so forth:

For their origins, there are very many explanations in the old translations:[131]

> It is the highest of protections and
> it cuts off rebirth in the six types [realms].
> It purifies the three transitional states,[132] and
> the spinning is of even greater purity than
> the mantra recitation itself;
> the benefits likewise are much greater.

There are no statements in the new tantras teaching the use of hand wheels. Still, several worthy and great persons have taken up the practice and spread it among all the monasteries of eastern and central Tibet. However, that in itself is not sufficient reason to hold it in esteem.

"The mantra of the tutelary spins quickly." Other passages exist on the circling of recitations of the wrathful deities and their vehicles; and many others that tell the way the letters of the mantras circle like lamps strung together. In the *Vajra Songs*, where it says, "It is good to turn a fast wheel," it teaches the need to turn the string of mantras in the heart center. Here we find the source for the practice of spinning external wheels that are inscribed [with mantras.][133]

The [outward] rituals for achieving the four actions[134] contained in the handbooks for the *sadhanas* of many particular deities and Dharma protectors, as well as the directions for inscribing the life circle, [all] agree with actual instructions for contemplation. The *Guhyasamaja Tantra* says, "The *Om* is…of a small chickpea-like pellet." The way of meditating on the inner substance as a "drop" is explained here and by many other authorities to be the source of outward pellet rites, understood in the conventional sense.[135]

The Fifth Dalai Lama's *Dharani Insertion* [Tib. *Zungzhug*] says that the source of [the practice of] winding about [the central axis] from the beginning [of the sacred text] is found in the [fact that] the beginning of the wheel of [visualized] mantras starts from the inside. Hence, if the contemplative visualization of an inward wheel of mantras lies at the origin of outward-inscribed wheels, then there can be no doubt that the teachings on turning a string of mantras [in visualizations] lie at the origin of the turning of external wheels.[136]

The contemplative visualizations [that one performs while spinning the wheel]: From whatever sutra or mantra may be enclosed, light emanates, and one offers worship to all the buddha realms. Their blessings coalesce and then melt within. Again, the light rays are emitted. They strike your own body. They purify the conscience[137] and all the obstacles to enlightenment, allowing the blessings of the buddhas and sons of buddhas to enter. Then the light rays spread throughout the universe to cleanse the biological and non-vital worlds of any impurity. Both the biological and non-vital worlds become pure. One imagines that all beings intone together the sutra or mantra, transmuting into a background continuity of spiritual suchness. In such manner, practicing the yogic training of body, speech, and mind, the individual letters [of the sutra or mantra] each utter their appropriate sounds, and one imagines that those who are capable of religious transformation are placed on the path of maturation and liberation. When this is done, one gains a connection to the turning of the wheel of Dharma [by a buddha].

The benefits of spinning the prayer wheel: It brings all the same benefits said to accrue from reading the respective texts. By writing one or more mantras on a slate and turning it a few times, one can openly stop contagions, frost, hail, and so forth. So, spinning a special mantra *dharani* several times with pure motivation can bring unimaginable benefits. Just being struck by a wind that has touched such a prayer wheel cleanses a great number of negativities and obstacles to enlightenment and is said to implant the seed of liberation.

Losang Samten, a faithful monk of the monastery of Kalka known as Khure Chenmo, impressed on me the need for a work on their rationale and benefits. So I, Reverend Konchog Tenpe Dronme, hastily composed this brief outline of topics relating to prayer wheels.

Dedication of Merits
From Building and Turning Prayer Wheels

The final translation is of a brief text written, as the colophon explains, as a dedication for the merits created by building wheels, turning mani wheels and reciting the mani mantra. Its author, Lama Ngawang Khedrub, later known as the Twelfth Abbot, Wagindra Patu Siddhi, was born in Mongolia in 1779, began his monastic education at Tashi Chopel College at Urga, and completed his Rabjampa Geshe degree at Drepung Monastic University in Central Tibet. He received his final ordination in the presence of the Eighth Dalai Lama. He then returned to Mongolia to become one of its leading teachers of the early nineteenth century. There, he also oversaw the completion of a large, gilt copper alloy image of Maitreya, the Buddha of Love.

Dan Martin first sent me a copy of this Tibetan text, which appears in an edition of the collected works of the author, reproduced under the instructions of Venerable Ling Rinpoche, the late senior tutor of His Holiness the Fourteenth Dalai Lama. The text was translated by Yeshe Kedrup and Wilson Hurley in Fairfax, Virginia in 1998, and it has since been used by Lama Zopa Rinpoche and others in blessing and dedicating prayer wheels large and small.

&A dedication prayer for the roots of virtue from building and spinning mani wheels is contained herein.

Om Svasti! (May all be well!)

By the blessings of all the buddhas, which depend upon the root and lineage lamas, the oceanic supreme three, and especially the supreme deity of compassion, the Compassionate-Eyed One, may the results of my prayers be accomplished exactly as wished.

The profound six-syllable mantra is the essence of all Dharma. May whatever virtues that have been collected in the three times through reciting it, building Dharma wheels, and so forth, never end, but always increase.

May this life's father and mother, my family, dependents, and myself all be held by spiritual guides and achieve perfect human lives through all of our future births. When our minds are ejected by death, may we be protected from the fears of lower realms by holding the supreme Three Refuges from the bottom of our hearts.

Through my subtle mind's realizing the system of causes and their effects, then making efforts at accepting virtuous deeds and rejecting evil deeds, and by always keeping the practice of the four powers, purification, and restraint, may the doors to evil-gone births always be blocked.

Even all of the happiness, fortune, and goodness of gods and men are just like the foods of many tastes enjoyed by evil spirits. Through the strong renunciation that comes from seeing this, may I make efforts in the three practices,[138] thereby reaching the fortress of the path of liberation.

All beings, equal to space, possess measureless kindness. By recognizing that each has been my mother, remembering their kindness to me, wishing to repay them, developing love for them and compassion, wishing to liberate them from all suffering, and through the extraordinary thought, may I generate the supreme mind that aspires for complete enlightenment.

All phenomena appear but have no self-existent nature. Holding the unwaning power of the essence of wisdom-compassion, realizing this emptiness, may I quickly achieve buddhahood through the practices of the six perfections, the four gatherings, and the two stages.

Temporarily, I will plant this Dharma wheel seed in the field of the transcendent ones, protected by the sunlight of the blessings of the Supreme Three. May it be held by the moisture of the compassion of the transcendent ones.

Moreover, may the power of spinning increase one hundred million times, like the strong trunk of a fully mature tree, from which the branches of the three doors' deeds benefiting others spread out with virtuous qualities in all directions, bringing satisfaction.

May countless light rays of compassion emanate from all the petals of the Dharma wheel's mantra syllables, purifying all the suffering and bad karma of the six realms and then establishing beings in the glory of benefit and happiness.

May the sound of the bells that hang from the Dharma wheel reflect the melody of the syllables of the profound heart mantra, and whoever's ears hear it—all beings—may it purify their bad karma and liberate them from lower realms.

May the leaves of life and virtue, a hundred thousand flowers of faith and morality, bloom with extreme beauty, and may the teachings and beings be nourished and completely filled by the taste of bodhichitta, the fruit of realization through practice.

When we are touched by the frost of winter, the Lord of Death, may the sun of the Transcendent Compassionate-Eyed One's good face directly appear, strengthening us with the moisture of powerful, virtuous minds, like faith and the rest, and may we be directly held by the Transcendent Compassionate-Eyed One's hand.

Unharmed by the ax blade of intense suffering and untainted by the touch of illusion's forest fire, while respectfully bowing the crown of our heads to the Transcendent Compassion Buddha's two feet, with the smiling flowers of joyful faith, may we be brought in.

In the joyful gardens of the Potala paradise and Sukhavati, by our seeds of birth ripening into the good race of Mahayana, may we develop the trunk of renunciation with limbs of bodhichitta-ripening fruit within a hundred thousand leaves and petals.

Nurtured by the rain of the Mahayana speech from Amitabha, the protector Maitreya, and the Compassionate-Eyed One, may the flower fields of the activities of bodhisattvas all bloom, proclaiming the fame of the buddhas.

By the jeweled net of divine vision and clairvoyance, may we bestow the glories of samsara and nirvana upon the minds of all beings, pervading all fields and realms with the fragrance of morality, and thereby taking away the suffering heat of karma and mental afflictions from all beings.

May the sounds of the three vehicles of Dharma bring its melodies of sweet songs to every being in every realm without exception, fitting their ears, awakening them from the sleep of ignorance, and joining them to the great celebration of the holy Dharma.

Like that, may the virtue of this effort, similar to a field of *sala* trees, gradually grow higher and increase until completely culminating, ripening into the fruit of the three bodies, like the clusters of grain at the tips of stalks, thereby nurturing all beings without exception.

May the shadow of these activities become equal to space, protecting the teachings and all beings until samsara ends through great compassion, like the Lord of Trees, and then may your minds and the minds of the divine beings join, becoming one.

Through the blessings of the excellent bodhisattvas and buddhas, the truth of the infallibility of dependent arising, and by the power of my exceptionally pure wishes, may the points of these pure prayers be accomplished.

The above was composed at the urging and request of the master of the faith, Tatushayay Gung Sonam Wangchuk. In Khure Chenmo, he collected the roots of virtue through a hundred million mani repetitions and twice building Dharma wheels. Some words of dedication were needed to dedicate the roots of virtue of these activities and the roots of virtue from spinning Dharma wheels. Therefore, this prayer was composed by the Twelfth Abbot, Wagindra Patu Siddhi, and written down by Prajnasakara. May goodness and virtue increase!

PART THREE:

*Diagrams, Pictures, and Instructions
for Prayer Wheel Construction*

&As the commentaries make clear, prayer wheels have been made in Tibet for centuries in a wide range of sizes. Some of these have been decorated very simply, with a metal, cloth, or leather covering. Others have inspired marvelous artwork. In recent decades, wherever Tibetan Buddhism has spread, people have gradually begun importing hand-held prayer wheels and even building large, artistically inspired prayer wheels.

Having purchased and examined hand-held and desktop prayer wheels from a wide range of stores and catalogs in Asia and in the West, I must caution the reader that such prayer wheels are rarely filled correctly. Instead, they are often filled with mantras or pictures printed unclearly or mantras inserted upside down, or even with a combination of mantras and old newsprint. This is often true even of prayer wheels sold at Buddhist centers. As the commentaries explain, the use of such improperly filled prayer wheels is unlikely to bring about the desired effects. Thus I urge practitioners to be sure that their prayer wheel was filled according to the instructions of a lama, or to purchase or make a prayer wheel and then fill it themselves according to the instructions in the traditional commentaries.

For those interested in the inner structure of a prayer wheel or in filling one, whether for their own use or the benefit of others, the following drawings, diagrams, and photos may be helpful. The instructions here conform to the method suggested by the Fourth Panchen Lama, which Lama Zopa Rinpoche has said is a correct method for filling mani wheels. At the suggestion of Zopa Rinpoche, photos of prayer wheels made with great artistry are also included. May these inform the reader and inspire future artists and artisans.

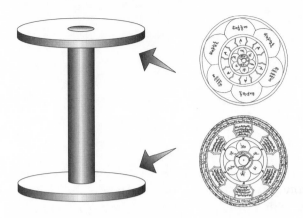

Filling the mani wheel—Step 1: Place the earth wheel inside the wheel, on the bottom facing up. The central shaft or "life-tree" of the prayer wheel passes through the circle at the center of the earth wheel. Similarly, attach the sky wheel inside to the top facing down with the central shaft passing through its center. [Earth and sky wheels prepared by Lama Zopa Rinpoche; see pp. 90–91.]

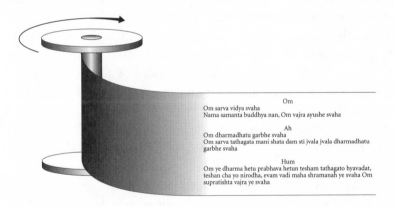

Om
Om sarva vidya svaha
Nama samanta buddhya nan, Om vajra ayushe svaha

Ah
Om dharmadhatu garbhe svaha
Om sarva tathagata mani shata dam sti jvala jvala dharmadhatu garbhe svaha

Hum
Om ye dharma hetu prabhava hetun tesham tathagato hyavadat, teshan cha yo nirodha, evam vadi maha shramanah ye svaha Om supratishta vajra ye svaha

Filling the mani wheel—Step 2: Bless the central shaft or "life-tree" of the prayer wheel by writing *Om, Ah,* and *Hum* on it and then writing the appropriate mantras beneath each of these syllables. These mantras can be written in Sanskrit, Tibetan (see page 92), or romanized script (see page 44). Also, they can be written on the central shaft or on paper and then wound on clockwise, facing out, as pictured here.

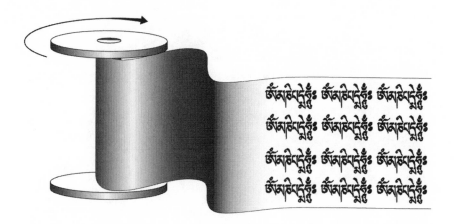

Filling the mani wheel—Step 3: Begin winding the pages of mani mantras into the prayer wheel. Following the method of the Fourth Panchen Lama, connect the side with the *Om* to the central shaft, with the mantras facing out, and then wind the mantras on clockwise until the prayer wheel is filled. At the end, one can wrap the mantras in cloth or paper of various colors as described in the commentaries.

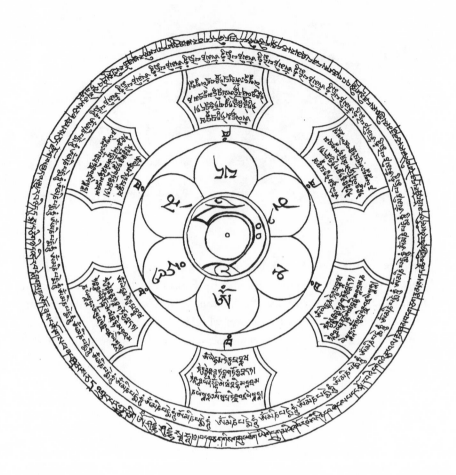

The earth wheel as drawn by Lama Zopa Rinpoche, following the instructions of the Fourth Panchen Lama. Place this inside the prayer wheel below the mani mantras, with the life-tree passing through the circle in the middle.

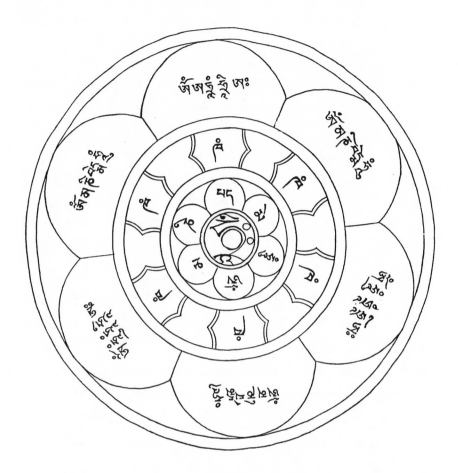

The sky wheel as drawn by Lama Zopa Rinpoche, following the instructions of the Fourth Panchen Lama. Place this inside the prayer wheel above the mani mantras, with the life-tree passing through the circle in the middle.

ཨོཾ

ཨོཾ་རཱ་བི་དྷུ་སྭཱ་ཧཱ། ཨོཾ་རཱ་བི་དྷུ་སྭཱ་ཧཱ། ཨོཾ་རཱ་བི་དྷུ་སྭཱ་ཧཱ། ཨོཾ་རཱ་བི་དྷུ་སྭཱ་ཧཱ། ཨོཾ་རཱ་བི་དྷུ་སྭཱ་ཧཱ། ཨོཾ་རཱ་བི་དྷུ་སྭཱ་ཧཱ། ཨོཾ་རཱ་བི་དྷུ་སྭཱ་ཧཱ། ཨོཾ་རཱ་བི་དྷུ་སྭཱ་ཧཱ།

ཨོཾ་རཱ་བི་དྷུ་སྭཱ་ཧཱ། ཨོཾ་རཱ་བི་དྷུ་སྭཱ་ཧཱ། ཨོཾ་རཱ་བི་དྷུ་སྭཱ་ཧཱ། ཨོཾ་རཱ་བི་དྷུ་སྭཱ་ཧཱ། ཨོཾ་རཱ་བི་དྷུ་སྭཱ་ཧཱ། ཨོཾ་རཱ་བི་དྷུ་སྭཱ་ཧཱ། ཨོཾ་རཱ་བི་དྷུ་སྭཱ་ཧཱ། ཨོཾ་རཱ་བི་དྷུ་སྭཱ་ཧཱ།

ཨོཾ་རཱ་བི་དྷུ་སྭཱ་ཧཱ། ཨོཾ་རཱ་བི་དྷུ་སྭཱ་ཧཱ། ཨོཾ་རཱ་བི་དྷུ་སྭཱ་ཧཱ། ཨོཾ་རཱ་བི་དྷུ་སྭཱ་ཧཱ། ཨོཾ་རཱ་བི་དྷུ་སྭཱ་ཧཱ། ཨོཾ་རཱ་བི་དྷུ་སྭཱ་ཧཱ། ཨོཾ་རཱ་བི་དྷུ་སྭཱ་ཧཱ། ཨོཾ་རཱ་བི་དྷུ་སྭཱ་ཧཱ།

ཨོཾ་རཱ་བི་དྷུ་སྭཱ་ཧཱ། ཨོཾ་རཱ་བི་དྷུ་སྭཱ་ཧཱ། ཨོཾ་རཱ་བི་དྷུ་སྭཱ་ཧཱ། ཨོཾ་རཱ་བི་དྷུ་སྭཱ་ཧཱ། ཨོཾ་རཱ་བི་དྷུ་སྭཱ་ཧཱ། ཨོཾ་རཱ་བི་དྷུ་སྭཱ་ཧཱ། ཨོཾ་རཱ་བི་དྷུ་སྭཱ་ཧཱ། ཨོཾ་རཱ་བི་དྷུ་སྭཱ་ཧཱ།

ན་མཿ་ས་མནྟ་བུདྡྷཱ་ནཱཾ། ཨོཾ་བཛྲ་ཨཱ་ཡུ་ཥེ་སྭཱ་ཧཱ། ན་མཿ་ས་མནྟ་བུདྡྷཱ་ནཱཾ། ཨོཾ་བཛྲ་ཨཱ་ཡུ་ཥེ་སྭཱ་ཧཱ། ན་མཿ་ས་མནྟ་བུདྡྷཱ་ནཱཾ། ཨོཾ་བཛྲ་ཨཱ་ཡུ་ཥེ་སྭཱ་ཧཱ། ན་མཿ་ས་མནྟ་བུདྡྷཱ་ནཱཾ།

ན་མཿ་ས་མནྟ་བུདྡྷཱ་ནཱཾ། ཨོཾ་བཛྲ་ཨཱ་ཡུ་ཥེ་སྭཱ་ཧཱ། ན་མཿ་ས་མནྟ་བུདྡྷཱ་ནཱཾ། ཨོཾ་བཛྲ་ཨཱ་ཡུ་ཥེ་སྭཱ་ཧཱ། ན་མཿ་ས་མནྟ་བུདྡྷཱ་ནཱཾ། ཨོཾ་བཛྲ་ཨཱ་ཡུ་ཥེ་སྭཱ་ཧཱ། ན་མཿ་ས་མནྟ་བུདྡྷཱ་ནཱཾ།

ན་མཿ་ས་མནྟ་བུདྡྷཱ་ནཱཾ། ཨོཾ་བཛྲ་ཨཱ་ཡུ་ཥེ་སྭཱ་ཧཱ། ན་མཿ་ས་མནྟ་བུདྡྷཱ་ནཱཾ། ཨོཾ་བཛྲ་ཨཱ་ཡུ་ཥེ་སྭཱ་ཧཱ། ན་མཿ་ས་མནྟ་བུདྡྷཱ་ནཱཾ། ཨོཾ་བཛྲ་ཨཱ་ཡུ་ཥེ་སྭཱ་ཧཱ། ན་མཿ་ས་མནྟ་བུདྡྷཱ་ནཱཾ།

ན་མཿ་ས་མནྟ་བུདྡྷཱ་ནཱཾ། ཨོཾ་བཛྲ་ཨཱ་ཡུ་ཥེ་སྭཱ་ཧཱ། ན་མཿ་ས་མནྟ་བུདྡྷཱ་ནཱཾ། ཨོཾ་བཛྲ་ཨཱ་ཡུ་ཥེ་སྭཱ་ཧཱ། ན་མཿ་ས་མནྟ་བུདྡྷཱ་ནཱཾ། ཨོཾ་བཛྲ་ཨཱ་ཡུ་ཥེ་སྭཱ་ཧཱ། ན་མཿ་ས་མནྟ་བུདྡྷཱ་ནཱཾ།

ཨཱཿ

ཨོཾ་རུ་རུ་ཏུ་ཏུ་གཉེ་སྭཱ་ཧཱ། ཨོཾ་རུ་རུ་ཏུ་ཏུ་གཉེ་སྭཱ་ཧཱ། ཨོཾ་རུ་རུ་ཏུ་ཏུ་གཉེ་སྭཱ་ཧཱ། ཨོཾ་རུ་རུ་ཏུ་ཏུ་གཉེ་སྭཱ་ཧཱ། ཨོཾ་རུ་རུ་ཏུ་ཏུ་གཉེ་སྭཱ་ཧཱ། ཨོཾ་རུ་རུ་ཏུ་ཏུ་གཉེ་སྭཱ་ཧཱ། ཨོཾ་རུ་རུ་ཏུ་ཏུ་གཉེ་སྭཱ་ཧཱ།

ཨོཾ་རུ་རུ་ཏུ་ཏུ་གཉེ་སྭཱ་ཧཱ། ཨོཾ་རུ་རུ་ཏུ་ཏུ་གཉེ་སྭཱ་ཧཱ། ཨོཾ་རུ་རུ་ཏུ་ཏུ་གཉེ་སྭཱ་ཧཱ། ཨོཾ་རུ་རུ་ཏུ་ཏུ་གཉེ་སྭཱ་ཧཱ། ཨོཾ་རུ་རུ་ཏུ་ཏུ་གཉེ་སྭཱ་ཧཱ། ཨོཾ་རུ་རུ་ཏུ་ཏུ་གཉེ་སྭཱ་ཧཱ། ཨོཾ་རུ་རུ་ཏུ་ཏུ་གཉེ་སྭཱ་ཧཱ།

ཨོཾ་རུ་རུ་ཏུ་ཏུ་གཉེ་སྭཱ་ཧཱ། ཨོཾ་རུ་རུ་ཏུ་ཏུ་གཉེ་སྭཱ་ཧཱ། ཨོཾ་རུ་རུ་ཏུ་ཏུ་གཉེ་སྭཱ་ཧཱ། ཨོཾ་རུ་རུ་ཏུ་ཏུ་གཉེ་སྭཱ་ཧཱ། ཨོཾ་རུ་རུ་ཏུ་ཏུ་གཉེ་སྭཱ་ཧཱ། ཨོཾ་རུ་རུ་ཏུ་ཏུ་གཉེ་སྭཱ་ཧཱ། ཨོཾ་རུ་རུ་ཏུ་ཏུ་གཉེ་སྭཱ་ཧཱ།

ཨོཾ་རུ་རུ་ཏུ་ཏུ་གཉེ་སྭཱ་ཧཱ། ཨོཾ་རུ་རུ་ཏུ་ཏུ་གཉེ་སྭཱ་ཧཱ། ཨོཾ་རུ་རུ་ཏུ་ཏུ་གཉེ་སྭཱ་ཧཱ། ཨོཾ་རུ་རུ་ཏུ་ཏུ་གཉེ་སྭཱ་ཧཱ། ཨོཾ་རུ་རུ་ཏུ་ཏུ་གཉེ་སྭཱ་ཧཱ། ཨོཾ་རུ་རུ་ཏུ་ཏུ་གཉེ་སྭཱ་ཧཱ། ཨོཾ་རུ་རུ་ཏུ་ཏུ་གཉེ་སྭཱ་ཧཱ།

ཧཱུྃ

At left: life-tree mantras. These mantras can be written directly on the central shaft of the prayer wheel or written on paper and then wrapped around the central shaft, clockwise, with the mantras facing out.

The following two pages are filled with mani mantras written in Tibetan script. These mantras, whether printed on paper or copied onto microfilm, can be used to completely fill the inside of a mani prayer wheel. The first page was prepared from an original sent from the office of His Holiness the Dalai Lama specifically for the purpose of filling mani wheels. The original was sent to Jim McCann, who was then working on prayer wheels at Land of Medicine Buddha in California. The original was scanned into a computer and reproduced to fill a page. It can be printed smaller to get more mani mantras on a page, as the commentaries indicate that the power of a prayer wheel is dependent on the number of mani mantras inside it. The second page was handwritten by Lama Zopa Rinpoche specifically for the purpose of filling mani wheels.

ༀ་མ་ཎི་པདྨེ་ཧཱུྃཿ ༀ་མ་ཎི་པདྨེ་ཧཱུྃཿ ༀ་མ་ཎི་པདྨེ་ཧཱུྃཿ ༀ་མ་ཎི་པདྨེ་ཧཱུྃཿ ༀ་མ་ཎི་པདྨེ་ཧཱུྃཿ ༀ་མ་ཎི་པདྨེ་ཧཱུྃཿ ༀ་མ་ཎི་པདྨེ་ཧཱུྃཿ ༀ་མ་ཎི་པདྨེ་ཧཱུྃཿ
ༀ་མ་ཎི་པདྨེ་ཧཱུྃཿ ༀ་མ་ཎི་པདྨེ་ཧཱུྃཿ ༀ་མ་ཎི་པདྨེ་ཧཱུྃཿ ༀ་མ་ཎི་པདྨེ་ཧཱུྃཿ ༀ་མ་ཎི་པདྨེ་ཧཱུྃཿ ༀ་མ་ཎི་པདྨེ་ཧཱུྃཿ ༀ་མ་ཎི་པདྨེ་ཧཱུྃཿ ༀ་མ་ཎི་པདྨེ་ཧཱུྃཿ
ༀ་མ་ཎི་པདྨེ་ཧཱུྃཿ ༀ་མ་ཎི་པདྨེ་ཧཱུྃཿ ༀ་མ་ཎི་པདྨེ་ཧཱུྃཿ ༀ་མ་ཎི་པདྨེ་ཧཱུྃཿ ༀ་མ་ཎི་པདྨེ་ཧཱུྃཿ ༀ་མ་ཎི་པདྨེ་ཧཱུྃཿ ༀ་མ་ཎི་པདྨེ་ཧཱུྃཿ ༀ་མ་ཎི་པདྨེ་ཧཱུྃཿ
ༀ་མ་ཎི་པདྨེ་ཧཱུྃཿ ༀ་མ་ཎི་པདྨེ་ཧཱུྃཿ ༀ་མ་ཎི་པདྨེ་ཧཱུྃཿ ༀ་མ་ཎི་པདྨེ་ཧཱུྃཿ ༀ་མ་ཎི་པདྨེ་ཧཱུྃཿ ༀ་མ་ཎི་པདྨེ་ཧཱུྃཿ ༀ་མ་ཎི་པདྨེ་ཧཱུྃཿ ༀ་མ་ཎི་པདྨེ་ཧཱུྃཿ
ༀ་མ་ཎི་པདྨེ་ཧཱུྃཿ ༀ་མ་ཎི་པདྨེ་ཧཱུྃཿ ༀ་མ་ཎི་པདྨེ་ཧཱུྃཿ ༀ་མ་ཎི་པདྨེ་ཧཱུྃཿ ༀ་མ་ཎི་པདྨེ་ཧཱུྃཿ ༀ་མ་ཎི་པདྨེ་ཧཱུྃཿ ༀ་མ་ཎི་པདྨེ་ཧཱུྃཿ ༀ་མ་ཎི་པདྨེ་ཧཱུྃཿ
ༀ་མ་ཎི་པདྨེ་ཧཱུྃཿ ༀ་མ་ཎི་པདྨེ་ཧཱུྃཿ ༀ་མ་ཎི་པདྨེ་ཧཱུྃཿ ༀ་མ་ཎི་པདྨེ་ཧཱུྃཿ ༀ་མ་ཎི་པདྨེ་ཧཱུྃཿ ༀ་མ་ཎི་པདྨེ་ཧཱུྃཿ ༀ་མ་ཎི་པདྨེ་ཧཱུྃཿ ༀ་མ་ཎི་པདྨེ་ཧཱུྃཿ
ༀ་མ་ཎི་པདྨེ་ཧཱུྃཿ ༀ་མ་ཎི་པདྨེ་ཧཱུྃཿ ༀ་མ་ཎི་པདྨེ་ཧཱུྃཿ ༀ་མ་ཎི་པདྨེ་ཧཱུྃཿ ༀ་མ་ཎི་པདྨེ་ཧཱུྃཿ ༀ་མ་ཎི་པདྨེ་ཧཱུྃཿ ༀ་མ་ཎི་པདྨེ་ཧཱུྃཿ ༀ་མ་ཎི་པདྨེ་ཧཱུྃཿ
ༀ་མ་ཎི་པདྨེ་ཧཱུྃཿ ༀ་མ་ཎི་པདྨེ་ཧཱུྃཿ ༀ་མ་ཎི་པདྨེ་ཧཱུྃཿ ༀ་མ་ཎི་པདྨེ་ཧཱུྃཿ ༀ་མ་ཎི་པདྨེ་ཧཱུྃཿ ༀ་མ་ཎི་པདྨེ་ཧཱུྃཿ ༀ་མ་ཎི་པདྨེ་ཧཱུྃཿ ༀ་མ་ཎི་པདྨེ་ཧཱུྃཿ
ༀ་མ་ཎི་པདྨེ་ཧཱུྃཿ ༀ་མ་ཎི་པདྨེ་ཧཱུྃཿ ༀ་མ་ཎི་པདྨེ་ཧཱུྃཿ ༀ་མ་ཎི་པདྨེ་ཧཱུྃཿ ༀ་མ་ཎི་པདྨེ་ཧཱུྃཿ ༀ་མ་ཎི་པདྨེ་ཧཱུྃཿ ༀ་མ་ཎི་པདྨེ་ཧཱུྃཿ ༀ་མ་ཎི་པདྨེ་ཧཱུྃཿ
ༀ་མ་ཎི་པདྨེ་ཧཱུྃཿ ༀ་མ་ཎི་པདྨེ་ཧཱུྃཿ ༀ་མ་ཎི་པདྨེ་ཧཱུྃཿ ༀ་མ་ཎི་པདྨེ་ཧཱུྃཿ ༀ་མ་ཎི་པདྨེ་ཧཱུྃཿ ༀ་མ་ཎི་པདྨེ་ཧཱུྃཿ ༀ་མ་ཎི་པདྨེ་ཧཱུྃཿ ༀ་མ་ཎི་པདྨེ་ཧཱུྃཿ
ༀ་མ་ཎི་པདྨེ་ཧཱུྃཿ ༀ་མ་ཎི་པདྨེ་ཧཱུྃཿ ༀ་མ་ཎི་པདྨེ་ཧཱུྃཿ ༀ་མ་ཎི་པདྨེ་ཧཱུྃཿ ༀ་མ་ཎི་པདྨེ་ཧཱུྃཿ ༀ་མ་ཎི་པདྨེ་ཧཱུྃཿ ༀ་མ་ཎི་པདྨེ་ཧཱུྃཿ ༀ་མ་ཎི་པདྨེ་ཧཱུྃཿ
ༀ་མ་ཎི་པདྨེ་ཧཱུྃཿ ༀ་མ་ཎི་པདྨེ་ཧཱུྃཿ ༀ་མ་ཎི་པདྨེ་ཧཱུྃཿ ༀ་མ་ཎི་པདྨེ་ཧཱུྃཿ ༀ་མ་ཎི་པདྨེ་ཧཱུྃཿ ༀ་མ་ཎི་པདྨེ་ཧཱུྃཿ ༀ་མ་ཎི་པདྨེ་ཧཱུྃཿ ༀ་མ་ཎི་པདྨེ་ཧཱུྃཿ
ༀ་མ་ཎི་པདྨེ་ཧཱུྃཿ ༀ་མ་ཎི་པདྨེ་ཧཱུྃཿ ༀ་མ་ཎི་པདྨེ་ཧཱུྃཿ ༀ་མ་ཎི་པདྨེ་ཧཱུྃཿ ༀ་མ་ཎི་པདྨེ་ཧཱུྃཿ ༀ་མ་ཎི་པདྨེ་ཧཱུྃཿ ༀ་མ་ཎི་པདྨེ་ཧཱུྃཿ ༀ་མ་ཎི་པདྨེ་ཧཱུྃཿ
ༀ་མ་ཎི་པདྨེ་ཧཱུྃཿ ༀ་མ་ཎི་པདྨེ་ཧཱུྃཿ ༀ་མ་ཎི་པདྨེ་ཧཱུྃཿ ༀ་མ་ཎི་པདྨེ་ཧཱུྃཿ ༀ་མ་ཎི་པདྨེ་ཧཱུྃཿ ༀ་མ་ཎི་པདྨེ་ཧཱུྃཿ ༀ་མ་ཎི་པདྨེ་ཧཱུྃཿ ༀ་མ་ཎི་པདྨེ་ཧཱུྃཿ
ༀ་མ་ཎི་པདྨེ་ཧཱུྃཿ ༀ་མ་ཎི་པདྨེ་ཧཱུྃཿ ༀ་མ་ཎི་པདྨེ་ཧཱུྃཿ ༀ་མ་ཎི་པདྨེ་ཧཱུྃཿ ༀ་མ་ཎི་པདྨེ་ཧཱུྃཿ ༀ་མ་ཎི་པདྨེ་ཧཱུྃཿ ༀ་མ་ཎི་པདྨེ་ཧཱུྃཿ ༀ་མ་ཎི་པདྨེ་ཧཱུྃཿ
ༀ་མ་ཎི་པདྨེ་ཧཱུྃཿ ༀ་མ་ཎི་པདྨེ་ཧཱུྃཿ ༀ་མ་ཎི་པདྨེ་ཧཱུྃཿ ༀ་མ་ཎི་པདྨེ་ཧཱུྃཿ ༀ་མ་ཎི་པདྨེ་ཧཱུྃཿ ༀ་མ་ཎི་པདྨེ་ཧཱུྃཿ ༀ་མ་ཎི་པདྨེ་ཧཱུྃཿ ༀ་མ་ཎི་པདྨེ་ཧཱུྃཿ
ༀ་མ་ཎི་པདྨེ་ཧཱུྃཿ ༀ་མ་ཎི་པདྨེ་ཧཱུྃཿ ༀ་མ་ཎི་པདྨེ་ཧཱུྃཿ ༀ་མ་ཎི་པདྨེ་ཧཱུྃཿ ༀ་མ་ཎི་པདྨེ་ཧཱུྃཿ ༀ་མ་ཎི་པདྨེ་ཧཱུྃཿ ༀ་མ་ཎི་པདྨེ་ཧཱུྃཿ ༀ་མ་ཎི་པདྨེ་ཧཱུྃཿ
ༀ་མ་ཎི་པདྨེ་ཧཱུྃཿ ༀ་མ་ཎི་པདྨེ་ཧཱུྃཿ ༀ་མ་ཎི་པདྨེ་ཧཱུྃཿ ༀ་མ་ཎི་པདྨེ་ཧཱུྃཿ ༀ་མ་ཎི་པདྨེ་ཧཱུྃཿ ༀ་མ་ཎི་པདྨེ་ཧཱུྃཿ ༀ་མ་ཎི་པདྨེ་ཧཱུྃཿ ༀ་མ་ཎི་པདྨེ་ཧཱུྃཿ
ༀ་མ་ཎི་པདྨེ་ཧཱུྃཿ ༀ་མ་ཎི་པདྨེ་ཧཱུྃཿ ༀ་མ་ཎི་པདྨེ་ཧཱུྃཿ ༀ་མ་ཎི་པདྨེ་ཧཱུྃཿ ༀ་མ་ཎི་པདྨེ་ཧཱུྃཿ ༀ་མ་ཎི་པདྨེ་ཧཱུྃཿ ༀ་མ་ཎི་པདྨེ་ཧཱུྃཿ ༀ་མ་ཎི་པདྨེ་ཧཱུྃཿ
ༀ་མ་ཎི་པདྨེ་ཧཱུྃཿ ༀ་མ་ཎི་པདྨེ་ཧཱུྃཿ ༀ་མ་ཎི་པདྨེ་ཧཱུྃཿ ༀ་མ་ཎི་པདྨེ་ཧཱུྃཿ ༀ་མ་ཎི་པདྨེ་ཧཱུྃཿ ༀ་མ་ཎི་པདྨེ་ཧཱུྃཿ ༀ་མ་ཎི་པདྨེ་ཧཱུྃཿ ༀ་མ་ཎི་པདྨེ་ཧཱུྃཿ
ༀ་མ་ཎི་པདྨེ་ཧཱུྃཿ ༀ་མ་ཎི་པདྨེ་ཧཱུྃཿ ༀ་མ་ཎི་པདྨེ་ཧཱུྃཿ ༀ་མ་ཎི་པདྨེ་ཧཱུྃཿ ༀ་མ་ཎི་པདྨེ་ཧཱུྃཿ ༀ་མ་ཎི་པདྨེ་ཧཱུྃཿ ༀ་མ་ཎི་པདྨེ་ཧཱུྃཿ ༀ་མ་ཎི་པདྨེ་ཧཱུྃཿ
ༀ་མ་ཎི་པདྨེ་ཧཱུྃཿ ༀ་མ་ཎི་པདྨེ་ཧཱུྃཿ ༀ་མ་ཎི་པདྨེ་ཧཱུྃཿ ༀ་མ་ཎི་པདྨེ་ཧཱུྃཿ ༀ་མ་ཎི་པདྨེ་ཧཱུྃཿ ༀ་མ་ཎི་པདྨེ་ཧཱུྃཿ ༀ་མ་ཎི་པདྨེ་ཧཱུྃཿ ༀ་མ་ཎི་པདྨེ་ཧཱུྃཿ
ༀ་མ་ཎི་པདྨེ་ཧཱུྃཿ ༀ་མ་ཎི་པདྨེ་ཧཱུྃཿ ༀ་མ་ཎི་པདྨེ་ཧཱུྃཿ ༀ་མ་ཎི་པདྨེ་ཧཱུྃཿ ༀ་མ་ཎི་པདྨེ་ཧཱུྃཿ ༀ་མ་ཎི་པདྨེ་ཧཱུྃཿ ༀ་མ་ཎི་པདྨེ་ཧཱུྃཿ ༀ་མ་ཎི་པདྨེ་ཧཱུྃཿ
ༀ་མ་ཎི་པདྨེ་ཧཱུྃཿ ༀ་མ་ཎི་པདྨེ་ཧཱུྃཿ ༀ་མ་ཎི་པདྨེ་ཧཱུྃཿ ༀ་མ་ཎི་པདྨེ་ཧཱུྃཿ ༀ་མ་ཎི་པདྨེ་ཧཱུྃཿ ༀ་མ་ཎི་པདྨེ་ཧཱུྃཿ ༀ་མ་ཎི་པདྨེ་ཧཱུྃཿ ༀ་མ་ཎི་པདྨེ་ཧཱུྃཿ
ༀ་མ་ཎི་པདྨེ་ཧཱུྃཿ ༀ་མ་ཎི་པདྨེ་ཧཱུྃཿ ༀ་མ་ཎི་པདྨེ་ཧཱུྃཿ ༀ་མ་ཎི་པདྨེ་ཧཱུྃཿ ༀ་མ་ཎི་པདྨེ་ཧཱུྃཿ ༀ་མ་ཎི་པདྨེ་ཧཱུྃཿ ༀ་མ་ཎི་པདྨེ་ཧཱུྃཿ ༀ་མ་ཎི་པདྨེ་ཧཱུྃཿ
ༀ་མ་ཎི་པདྨེ་ཧཱུྃཿ ༀ་མ་ཎི་པདྨེ་ཧཱུྃཿ ༀ་མ་ཎི་པདྨེ་ཧཱུྃཿ ༀ་མ་ཎི་པདྨེ་ཧཱུྃཿ ༀ་མ་ཎི་པདྨེ་ཧཱུྃཿ ༀ་མ་ཎི་པདྨེ་ཧཱུྃཿ ༀ་མ་ཎི་པདྨེ་ཧཱུྃཿ ༀ་མ་ཎི་པདྨེ་ཧཱུྃཿ

The mantra in Landzha script. The mantra in golden letters of this script typically decorates the outside of the mani wheel.

The Landzha mani on a large prayer wheel near Bouddha Stupa in Kathmandu, Nepal. The eight auspicious symbols adorn the wheel above the mantra. [Photo courtesy of Ven. Roger Kunsang]

Mantras on microfilm that have been wound around metal tubing, about to be placed around the metal life-tree of a handheld prayer wheel. In this case, the life-tree mantras were wrapped around the tubing and then the microfilm was wrapped on and sealed in place with colored tape.
[Photo courtesy of Venerable Paula Chichester]

The inside of a simple, desktop prayer wheel given to the editor by his friend, Ngawangthondup Narkyid. Made by Tibetans in exile in India from recycled materials—a coffee can and a drill bit—the wheel turns easily and steadily by resting in a halved peach pit set in a bit of concrete at the bottom of the wheel.
[Photo courtesy of Gerry Gomez]

A drawing of the interior of a large prayer wheel similar to the one made by Jim McCann at Land of Medicine Buddha in California. In this case, mantras on microfilm are wound into large disks the size of the prayer wheel, with a center hollow and large enough for the prayer wheel's life-tree to fit through. The disks are then stacked inside, filling the wheel entirely.
[Drawing by Anthony Thomas, design by Jim McCann]

Thousand-arm Avalokiteshvara, the Compassion Buddha.
[Drawing by Robert Beer]

Lama Zopa Rinpoche with a standing, handcrafted, silver desktop prayer wheel. The ornate silver casing remains stationary, as mantras are spun internally via the silver knob on top. [Photo courtesy of Jan-Paul Kool]

Kirti Tsenshab Rinpoche turns the desktop prayer wheel as Lama Zopa Rinpoche looks on. [Photo courtesy of Venerable Roger Kunsang]

A handheld prayer wheel made by Lama Zopa Rinpoche for his mother. The wheel is made of silver, and the eight auspicious symbols appear between the letters of the mani mantra. [Photo courtesy of Sangay Sherpa]

The editor using a handheld prayer wheel.

A revolving bookcase in Japan. [Photo courtesy of Robert Jones]

A woman in Nepal stands by a prayer wheel. [Photo courtesy of Venerable Roger Kunsang]

A nun spins a prayer wheel at Boudhanath, Kathmandu, Nepal. [Photo courtesy of Venerable Roger Kunsang]

A large prayer wheel in Nepal. [Photo courtesy of Venerable Roger Kunsang]

A large prayer wheel in Pokhara, Nepal. [Photo courtesy of Venerable Roger Kunsang]

A large prayer wheel at Chenrezig Institute, Queensland, Australia. [Photo courtesy of Venerable Roger Kunsang]

A prayer wheel at Land of Medicine Buddha, Soquel, California, at its consecration ceremony. The creator of the prayer wheel, Jim McCann, stands behind. The wheel has been decorated more elaborately since this photo was taken. [Photo courtesy of Venerable Roger Kunsang]

Above: After consecrating it, Lama Zopa Rinpoche stands next to another prayer wheel at Land of Medicine Buddha in Soquel, California. At the time of the photo, the wheel had been filled, but as with the wheel in the previous photo, there has since been additional work done on the outside decoration.

Left: Lama Zopa Rinpoche makes good use of long van ride.

[Photos courtesy of Venerable Roger Kunsang]

PART FOUR:

A Method for Meditating with the Prayer Wheel

A METHOD FOR MEDITATING WITH THE PRAYER WHEEL

HOMAGE TO THE GURU, TRANSCENDENT AVALOKITESHVARA, THE BUDDHA OF COMPASSION.

Om Mani Padme Hum

REFUGE AND BODHICHITTA MOTIVATION

(Recite 3 times)

I go to refuge until I am enlightened to the Buddha, the Dharma, and the Supreme Assembly.
By the virtuous merit that I create by practicing giving and the other perfections,
may I attain the state of a buddha in order to benefit all sentient beings.

RECALL:

The purpose of my life is to not just to find happiness for myself and to solve all of my own problems. The purpose of my life is to free the numberless sentient beings, making myself useful and beneficial to them. I will free each of them from all their sufferings and lead them to happiness in this life, happiness in future lives, perfect rebirths, the ultimate happiness of liberation from samsara, and then the peerless happiness of full enlightenment.

VISUALIZATION & RECITATION

Begin turning the mani wheel clockwise and reciting the mantra: *Om mani padme hum.* While continuing to turn the wheel and recite the mantra, go through the following visualizations, spending as much time on each as possible.

PURIFYING YOURSELF

Beams of light are emitted from the mani wheel, drawing out all of your negative karma, as well as all disturbing thoughts and all obscurations. These take the form of darkness, which is completely absorbed into the mani wheel and then destroyed.

As the beams continue to radiate, you develop love, compassion, equanimity, joy, and bodhichitta. You complete the practice of the six perfections, and you become like the Compassion Buddha, completely dedicated to the welfare of all sentient beings.

PURIFYING HELL-BEINGS

Beams of light are emitted from the mani wheel, drawing out all of the sufferings of the beings in the hell realms—such as experiencing unbearable heat or cold, being crushed alive, being boiled, and being cut or beaten. The light beams also draw out all of their negative karma, as well as disturbing thoughts, such as anger, and all obscurations. All of the negativity takes the form of darkness, which is completely absorbed into the mani wheel and destroyed. As the beams continue to radiate, all these beings develop love, compassion, equanimity, joy, and bodhichitta. They complete the practice of the six perfections. They attain the fully enlightened state of the Compassion Buddha.

PURIFYING HUNGRY GHOSTS

Beams of light are emitted from the mani wheel, drawing out all of the sufferings of the beings in realms of the hungry ghosts—such as unbearable hunger and thirst, inability to find or take in sustenance, exhaustion, fear, and heat or cold. The light beams also draw out all of their negative karma, as well as disturbing thoughts, such as greed and all obscurations. All of the negativity takes the form of darkness, which is completely absorbed into the mani wheel and then destroyed.

As the beams continue to radiate, all these beings develop love, compassion, equanimity, joy, and bodhichitta. They complete the practice of the six perfections. They attain the fully enlightened state of the Compassion Buddha.

PURIFYING ANIMALS

Beams of light are emitted from the mani wheel, drawing out all of the sufferings of the beings in the animal realms—such as being attacked and eaten by others, being imprisoned or forced to work by humans, illnesses, heat or cold, fear, and stupidity. The light beams also draw out all of their negative karma, as well as disturbing thoughts, such as ignorance, and all obscurations. All of the negativity takes the form of darkness, which is completely absorbed into the mani wheel and then destroyed.

As the beams continue to radiate, all these beings develop love, compassion, equanimity, joy, and bodhichitta. They complete the practice of the six perfections. They attain the fully enlightened state of the Compassion Buddha.

PURIFYING HUMANS

Beams of light are emitted from the mani wheel, drawing out all of the sufferings of the beings in the human realm—such as not getting what one wants, losing what one has, anxiety, depression, poverty, war, illness, and death. The light beams also draw out all of their negative karma, disturbing thoughts such as desire, as well as all obscurations. All of the negativity takes the form of darkness, which is completely absorbed into the mani wheel and then destroyed.

As the beams continue to radiate, all these beings develop love, compassion, equanimity, joy, and bodhichitta. They complete the practice of the six perfections. They attain the fully enlightened state of the Compassion Buddha.

PURIFYING DEMIGODS

Beams of light are emitted from the mani wheel, drawing out all of the sufferings of the beings in the demigod realm—such as unbearable jealousy of the gods, mental agitation, fighting, and losing in battle with the gods. The light beams also draw out all of their negative karma, disturbing thoughts such as jealousy, as well as all obscurations. All of the negativity takes the form of darkness, which is completely absorbed into the mani wheel and then destroyed.

As the beams continue to radiate, all these beings develop love, compassion, equanimity, joy, and bodhichitta. They complete the practice of the six perfections. They attain the fully enlightened state of the Compassion Buddha.

PURIFYING GODS

Beams of light are emitted from the mani wheel, drawing out all of the sufferings of the beings in the god realms—such as remaining in samsara due to one's delusions and disturbing thoughts, still having to fear rebirth in the lower realms, and the terrible suffering of death. The light beams also draw out all of their negative karma, disturbing thoughts such as pride, as well as all obscurations. All of the negativity takes the form of darkness, which is completely absorbed into the mani wheel and then destroyed.

As the beams continue to radiate, all these beings develop love, compassion, equanimity, joy, and bodhichitta. They complete the practice of the six perfections. They attain the fully enlightened state of the Compassion Buddha.

PURIFYING BEINGS IN THE INTERMEDIATE STATE

Beams of light are emitted from the mani wheel, drawing out all of the sufferings of the beings who have recently died and are now in the intermediate state. The light beams also draw out all of their negative karma, as well as all disturbing thoughts and all obscurations. All of the negativity takes the form of darkness, which is completely absorbed into the mani wheel and then destroyed.

As the beams continue to radiate, all these beings develop love, compassion, equanimity, joy, and bodhichitta. They complete the practice of the six perfections. They attain the fully enlightened state of the Compassion Buddha.

DEDICATION

By this virtue may I quickly attain the state of the Buddha of Compassion and lead all beings without exception to that enlightened state.

May the supreme jewel, bodhichitta, that has not arisen, arise and grow; and may that which has arisen not diminish, but increase more and more.

May the lives of those compassionate ones who've embodied in human form—His Holiness the Dalai Lama, the virtuous friends, and all holy beings—remain long and stable.

As a result of these merits, by merely seeing, hearing, touching, talking with, or thinking of me, may any being be freed immediately from all sufferings, diseases, spirit harms, negative karma, disturbing thoughts, and all obscurations, and may they abide in the peerless happiness of full enlightenment forever.

SUMMARY OF BENEFITS

The mani wheel particularly helps one to develop great compassion and bodhichitta; it helps one to complete the accumulation of extensive merit and purify obscurations so as to achieve enlightenment as quickly as possible.

The mani wheel embodies all the actions of the buddhas and bodhisattvas of the ten directions. To benefit sentient beings, the buddhas and bodhisattvas manifest in the mani wheel in order to purify all of our negative karma and all obscurations, and to cause us to actualize the realizations of the path to enlightenment. All the numberless beings in the area where the mani wheel is built, are saved

from rebirth in the lower realms; they receive a godly or human body, or are born in a pure land of Buddha. If you have a mani wheel in your house, your house is the same as the Potala, the pure land of the Compassion Buddha. If you have a mani wheel next to you when you die, that itself becomes a method to transfer your consciousness to the pure land of Buddha Amitabha or of the Compassion Buddha. Simply touching a mani wheel brings great purification of negative karma and obscurations.

Anyone who recites the six syllables while turning the Dharma wheel at the same time is equal in fortune to the Thousand Buddhas.

Turning the Dharma wheel is better than listening, reflecting, and meditating for aeons.

Turning the Dharma wheel once is better than attempting to practice the ten transcendent perfections for a thousand years. It is even better than explaining and listening to the Three Baskets and the four tantras for aeons.

A person who turns the Dharma wheel will gain mastery in relation to human beings, wealth, and sustenance. Just seeing such a person will benefit others with whom there is a connection. Sentient beings who are touched by such a person's shadow will be liberated from the lower realms.

This practice purifies the five uninterrupted karmas and the ten nonvirtuous actions; it purifies all evil-gone actions, which are causes of rebirth in the lower realms.

One will receive the blessings from the lineage lamas and have one's wishes miraculously fulfilled by the mind-seal deities. One will naturally fulfill the Buddhas' thoughts. Also, dakas and dakinis (male and female angels) will eliminate one's obstacles. The protector-deities will act according to one's wishes.

Even those lacking perseverance in their practice, who pass the time passively, will be able to attain mystic powers. Those with perseverance for reciting the mantra and turning the wheel will undoubtedly attain the highest bodhisattva level.

Even if one has no thought to benefit oneself, encouraging another to write the mantra and turn the wheel eliminates your negativity and completes your good qualities.

Not knowing the practice of the Dharma wheel and relying upon other practices is like a blind person trying to see—there is no way to succeed. A person with small wisdom and great laziness is like a donkey sunk in mud. Therefore cherish the practice of the Dharma wheel.

Notes

1 Mahayana (Great Vehicle) Buddhism is distinguished from Hinayana (Lower Vehicle) Buddhism based on the motivation of the practitioner. For a practitioner to be engaged in Mahayana Buddhist practice, he or she must, based on great compassion and altruism, give rise to bodhichitta—the mind that aspires to become a buddha in order to free all sentient beings from suffering.

2 D.T. Suzuki, *Manual of Zen Buddhism* (New York: Grove Press, 1961), p. 35.

3 Lama Zopa Rinpoche, *The Door to Satisfaction* (Boston: Wisdom Publications, 1994), pp. 7, 37.

4 Shantideva, *Siksa-Samuccaya: A Compendium of Buddhist Doctrine*, trans. Cecil Bendall & W.H.D. Rouse (Delhi: Motilal Banarsidass, 1922), p. 271.

5 Tantrayana, or Vajrayana, Buddhism is a subset of Mahayana Buddhism. It offers additional methods that allow the practitioner, when practicing under the guidance of a qualified lama, to progress much more quickly toward the goal of buddhahood for the sake of others.

6 For more detailed instructions on taking-and-giving meditation, see *Liberation in the Palm of Your Hand* by Pabongka Rinpoche or *Advice From a Spiritual Friend* by Geshe Rabten and Geshe Dhargyey (Boston: Wisdom Publications, 1996).

7 Pabongka Rinpoche, *Liberation in the Palm of Your Hand*, ed. Trijang Rinpoche, trans. Michael Richards (Boston: Wisdom Publications, 1991), p. 599.

8 Tsong-ka-pa, *Tantra In Tibet: The Great Exposition of Secret Mantra*, trans. & ed. Jeffrey Hopkins (London: George Allen & Unwin Publishers, 1977), p. 47.

9 Kalu Rinpoche, *Gently Whispered*, ed. E. Selandia (Barrytown, NY: Station Hill Press, 1994) pp. 106–13.

10 Dilgo Khyentse Rinpoche, *The Heart Treasure of the Enlightened Ones*, trans. Padmakara Translation Group (Boston: Shambhala Publications, 1992), p. 89.

11 Herbert Benson, *The Relaxation Response* (New York: William Morrow, 1975).

12 K.R. Eppley, A.I. Abrams, & J. Shear, "Differential Effects of Relaxation Techniques on Trait Anxiety: A Meta-Analysis," *Journal of Clinical Psychology*, 45: pp. 957–74.

13 Kalu Rinpoche, pp. 107–8.

14 Lama Thubten Yeshe, *The Tantric Path of Purification* (Boston: Wisdom Publications, 1995), pp. 61–62.

15 Dilgo Khentse Rinpoche, p. 89.

16 Robert Thurman & Tad Wise, *Circling the Sacred Mountain* (New York: Bantam Books, 1999), p. 318.

17 See His Holiness The Fourteenth Dalai Lama's *Kindness, Clarity and Insight* (Ithaca: Snow Lion Publications, 1984), pp. 116–17, for a brief but interesting commentary on the meaning of the mani mantra.

18 As quoted in "The Benefits of the Six-Syllable Essence Mantra," published in Tibetan by Sri Ngawang Jigmey, Lall Market Road, in Gangtok, Sikkim. Trans. by David Molk.

19 Dilgo Khyentse Rinpoche, p. 58.

20 Lama Thubten Yeshe, *Introduction to Tantra: A Vision of Totality* (Boston: Wisdom Publications, 1987), p. 32.

21 Ibid., p. 46.

22 Ibid., p. 42.

23 Delog Dawa Drolma, *Delog: Journey to the Realms Beyond Death* (Junction City, CA: Padma Publishing, 1995), p. 59.

24 J.E. Cirlot, *A Dictionary of Symbols*, trans. J. Sage (New York: Barnes & Noble Books, 1971), p. 370.

25 Dagyab Rinpoche, *Buddhist Symbols*, trans. Maurice Walshe (Boston: Wisdom Publications, 1995), p. 30.

26 Tsonghapa & Pabongka Rinpoche, *Preparing for Tantra: The Mountain of Blessings*, trans. Khen Rinpoche & Michael Roach (Howell, NJ: Mahayana Sutra & Tantra Press, 1995), p. 21.

27 Shakti M. Gupta, *Surya the Sun God* (Bombay: Somaiya Publications, 1977), p. 4.

28 William Simpson, *The Buddhist Praying Wheel* (New Hyde Park, NY: University Books, 1970), p. 45. Simpson asserts that the tradition of the *chakravartin* is rooted in even earlier myths regarding Surya, the sun god. The theme of seeing

a king as a representative of the divine (and of a solar divinity in particular) is common to a number of cultures and times.

29 Elie Wiesel, *Sages and Dreamers* (New York: Simon & Schuster, 1991), p. 89.

30 The similarities between Ezekiel's vision and the prayer wheel material is also striking in that one of the angels with a wheel is described as having the face of a lion, and the prayer wheel commentaries describe Nagarjuna giving the prayer wheel to a *dakini*—an angelic being—with a lion face.

31 John Strong, *The Legend of King Asoka: A Study of the Asokavadana* (Princeton: Princeton University Press, 1983), p. 46. Strong also notes how by the time of the Buddha, four kinds of wheel-turning kings were described; one for whom a golden wheel appears is said to have the most virtue and power, followed by those with silver, copper, and iron wheels.

32 From *Mindful Establishment of the Excellent Dharma*. This section was translated in the context of a discussion of the symbolism of the wheel in Dagyab Rinpoche's *Buddhist Symbols*, pp. 67–68.

33 Glenn Mullin, *Selected Works of the Dalai Lama I: Bridging the Sutras and Tantras* (Ithaca: Snow Lion Publications, 1981), p. 55.

34 Ibid.

35 Gupta, p. 8.

36 Gupta, p. 21.

37 Thomas Cleary, trans., *The Flower Ornament Scripture* (Boston: Shambhala Publications, 1985), p. 443.

38 Lama Govinda, *The Psycho-Cosmic Symbolism of the Buddhist Stupa* (Emeryville, CA: Dharma Publishing, 1976), pp. 80–81. "Liberation" in this context refers to the Buddha's death—his passing away into final nirvana.

39 Simpson, pp. 90–91.

40 Barry Bryant, *The Wheel of Time Sand Mandala* (San Francisco: HarperCollins, 1993), p. 21. The mandalas of Tibetan Buddhism, such as the sand mandalas that monks have made in art museums around the world, symbolize, through tantric deities and their palaces, the fully enlightened mind.

41 Cleary, p. 359.

42 Bryant, p. 257.

43 Robert Thurman, *The Central Philosophy of Tibet: A Study and Translation of Jey Tsong Khapa's Essence of True Eloquence* (Princeton: Princeton University

Press, 1984), p. 23. Thurman describes nagas as "mythic dragonlike beings from the depths of the ocean, whose magic powers included the ability to assume human form when visiting among humans." There is no English term that fully captures the complexity of the Indo-Tibetan associations with the term *naga.* "Dragon," "serpent," and "serpent-spirit" have each been used at times to capture some portion of these associations.

44 Robert Thurman, foreword to Lex Hixon's *Mother of the Buddhas* (Wheaton, IL: Quest Books, 1993), p. xi.

45 Thurman, *The Central Philosophy of Tibet,* p. 23. Dowman notes that Nagarjuna's biography agrees with this prophecy of Nagarjuna's rebirth in the land of bliss [Skt. *Sukhavati*], noting that his last words were "I go to Sukhavati, but I will return to this body." From Keith Dowman, *Masters of Mahamudra* (Albany: State University of New York Press, 1985), p. 119.

46 This account of Nagarjuna's life is based primarily on accounts from Robert Thurman and on Keith Dowman. See sources noted above.

47 Dowman, pp. 112–14.

48 *Dharmacakra* here means "wheel of Dharma." Nagarjuna is referring to turning the wheel of Dharma as the Buddha himself did. As previously noted, there is a resonance here between turning the wheel of Dharma and turning the Dharma or prayer wheel.

49 *Bodhi* here can be translated as "awakening" or "enlightenment." A buddha is one who has attained bodhi. So, by acting with great compassion and working for the sake of others, enlightenment falls directly into one's hands. The title of the text from which this quote is taken, *The [Two] Collections for Enlightenment* [Skt. *Bodhisambhara*], indicates that one must collect great merit (by acting with compassion) and great wisdom in order to achieve bodhi, or enlightenment.

50 Christian Lindtner, *Nagarjuniana: Studies in the Writings and Philosophy of Nagarjuna* (Delhi: Motilal Banarsidass Publishers, 1982), p. 233.

51 Nagarjuna & Kaysang Gyatso, *The Precious Garland and the Song of the Four Mindfulnesses* (New York: Harper & Row, 1975), p. 90.

52 Thurman, in his foreword to *Mother of the Buddhas,* notes that these teachings were entrusted to the "dragons and recovered only after four centuries." He says that this was because "the developing societies of" India needed hundreds of "years of preparation and purification" through the practice of the Buddha's teachings on "monastic education and renunciative ethic[s]" to be prepared for the "profound liberation of the teaching of voidness and the magnificent energization of the vision of the jeweline Buddhaverse," as taught

in the sutras discovered by Nagarjuna. In *The Central Philosophy of Tibet*, Thurman notes that by the first century B.C.E., the "time was ripe for the Universal Vehicle," or Mahayana, with its emphasis on "the solidarity of brotherhood and universal love and compassion." He also notes that this "great stream of love and compassion," which flowed from "the *naga* kingdom" through India to much of Central and East Asia, was roughly contemporaneous with another that flowed from Jesus in the Middle East through much of the Western world.

53 See Thurman's *The Central Philosophy of Tibet*, pp. 24–27 and Thurman's foreword to *Mother of the Buddhas*, p. xii.

54 The Seventh Dalai Lama, *Nyung Nä*, trans. Lama Zopa Rinpoche & George Churinoff (Boston: Wisdom Publications, 1995), p. 195.

55 Taranatha, *Taranatha's History of Buddhism in India*, trans. L. Chimpa & A. Chattopadhyaya (Delhi: Motilal Banarsidass Publishers, 1970), p. 112.

56 Martin Willson, *In Praise of Tara: Songs to the Savioress* (Boston: Wisdom Publications, 1986), p. 186.

57 Ibid., p. 398.

58 L.C. Goodrich, "The Revolving Bookcase in China," *Harvard Journal of Asiatic Studies*, VII (1942): p. 159.

59 For more on the early history of Buddhism in Tibet, see Dudjom Rinpoche, *The Nyingma School of Tibetan Buddhism* (Boston: Wisdom Publications, 1991).

60 James O. Caswell asserts that the idea of clockwise circumambulation came to China from India in *Written and Unwritten: A New History of the Buddhist Caves at Yungang*. This suggests an Indian origin for a practice involving clockwise turning of the wheel, as does the relevant Tibetan literature. Some Chinese sources also suggest that this practice came from India.

61 According to L.C. Goodrich, a number of early revolving bookcases in China were built in temples alongside statues of Avalokiteshvara, suggesting some early awareness of a link between the revolving bookcase and the Buddha of Compassion. Goodrich, pp. 130–64. A prayer from a Korean Zen Monastery translated by Buswell that was "composed in literary Chinese" and is clearly derived from Sanskrit sources is suggestive in this regard (Robert E. Buswell, *The Zen Monastic Experience* (Princeton: Princeton University Press, 1992)). A number of Sanskrit mantras and *dharanis*, including the mani mantra, appear within it. This prayer contains a beautiful section in which one imagines oneself, empowered by Avalokiteshvara, going to each of the lower realms—the hell, hungry ghost, and animal realms—and causing all suffering to spontaneously cease in each. This practice is remarkably similar to the visualization

done in the prayer wheel practice. This same Korean Zen prayer also pays homage to Avalokiteshvara as a bodhisattva "Contemplating the Sound of the World," as a "Great Wheel," and most intriguingly, as a "Wish-Fulfilling Jewel Wheel." Regarding this last reference, the translator of the prayer includes the Sanskrit name for this type of homage: *chintamanichakra*, that is, wish-fulfilling mani wheel. (Cf. Robert E. Buswell, *The Zen Monastic Experience* (Princeton: Princeton University Press, 1992), p. 238.) Note that there is a particular manifestation or form of Avalokiteshvara that appears in a number of Chinese and Japanese paintings called *Chintamanichakra*. Alice Getty, in *The Gods of Northern Buddhism*, observes that later Japanese images of this form of Avalokiteshvara picture him holding a wish-fulfilling jewel [Skt. *chintamani*] in one hand and a wheel in another, thus accounting for the name. However, an intriguing passage in *Taranatha's History of Buddhism in India* suggests another possibility. Taranatha describes an eighth-century Indian Buddhist pandit named Jñanagarbha, who "propitiated" Avalokiteshvara for a long time and then "at last had a vision of him as moving the *Chintamanichakra* and attained *abhijnana*." That Jñanagarbha's vision was of Avalokiteshvara *moving* the wish-fulfilling mani wheel suggests the possibility that this term in its original Indian usage may have referred to a prayer wheel rather than a separate form of the deity.

62 Yeshe De Project, *Dharma Wheel Cutting Karma* (Berkeley: Dharma Publishing, 1994).

63 These three deities are often grouped together, as Avalokiteshvara embodies the buddhas' compassion, Manjushri their wisdom, and Vajrapani their power.

64 "On the Origin and Significance of the Prayer Wheel According to Two Nineteenth-Century Tibetan Literary Sources," *The Journal of the Tibet Society*, VII (1987), p. 20.

65 G.N. Roerich, trans., *The Blue Annals* (New Delhi: Motilal Banarsidass, 1949), pp. 693–94.

66 Shabkar, *The Life of Shabkar*, trans. Matthieu Ricard (Albany: State University of New York Press, 1994), p. 525.

67 Lynn White, *Medieval Religion and Technology* (Berkeley: University of California Press, 1978), p. 50.

68 E. R. Huc, *Travels in Tartary*, trans. W. Hazlitt (New York: Alfred A. Knopf Publishers, 1927). Like many early travelers, Huc was clearly suspicious of the many methods of prayer he observed in Tibet. Unfortunately, language barriers prevented these early travelers from ever asking the Tibetans themselves what their rituals signified.

69 Well known to Westerners as the Mount Everest region of Nepal, Solu Kumbu is the birthplace of Lama Zopa Rinpoche.

70 In fact, Lama Zopa Rinpoche is widely accepted as the reincarnation of the previous Lawudo Lama, making him the current Lawudo Lama.

71 *Phowa* is a practice designed to help a dying person transfer his or her consciousness to a pure realm at the time of death.

72 The Buddha of Compassion referred to here is Avalokiteshvara. The term *six-syllable* refers to Avalokiteshvara's mantra which has six syllables: *Om mani padme hum.*

73 Tibetan texts often begin as this one does, with a Sanskrit line of praise. In this way, the Tibetan author paid homage to the Indian masters from whom the lineage of the subject matter of the text was derived. The line of homage beginning this text may be translated, "Homage to the Transcendent Master Avalokiteshvara."

74 The "two collections" are the collection of merit, or virtue, and the collection of wisdom. Both are necessary for enlightenment.

75 The "degenerate age" or [Skt. *Kaliyuga*] is an age during which negativity grows strong and the Buddha's Dharma declines; ours is considered such an age.

76 That is, the thousand buddhas of our current eon. The Mahayana Buddhist tradition holds that a thousand buddhas will appear on the earth in supreme emanation bodies to lead beings during this eon. For this reason, ours is considered a particularly auspicious eon. Buddha Shakyamuni is the fourth of these thousand buddhas to appear. Kashyapa was the buddha who appeared prior to Shakyamuni, and Maitreya, the Buddha of Love, will be the next to come.

77 Though our current text does not indicate the source for this quotation, the *Benefits of the Lotus Wheel,* sections of which appear in translation later in this book, indicates that this quote comes from a sutra entitled *Great River.*

78 The name of the person the Buddha is addressing here, Dikpa Namsel, means "completely eliminating obscurations."

79 The "ten perfections" [Skt. *paramitas*] are the practices that a bodhisattva engages in while striving for buddhahood. The ten perfections are generosity, ethical discipline, patience, joyous effort, concentration, wisdom, skillful means, prayer, power, and pristine cognition. The first six are often referred to as the "six perfections."

80 The *tripitaka* are the "three baskets" of Buddhist teachings—the vinaya, the sutras, and the abidharma. The "four tantras" refer to the four classes of

tantra—action tantra, performance tantra, yoga tantra, and highest yoga tantra. For a complete discussion of this subject, see Tsong-ka-pa, *Tantra in Tibet*, ed. & trans. Jeffrey Hopkins (London: George Allen & Unwin, 1977).

81 The "hook" here probably refers to the hook for attaching the counterweight to a wheel.

82 *Asura* is the Sanskrit term for a class of beings who live in heaven-like realms and have more power and wealth than humans but less than the gods [Skt. *devas*]. These *asuras* are prone to intense jealousy and fighting. *Yaksha* is the Sanskrit term for a demonic sort of being. Terry Clifford translates *yaksha* as "harm-giver." "They haunt mountain passes and similar places and are sometimes called direction-demons," he says, and "they often cause harm." See Terry Clifford, *Tibetan Buddhist Medicine and Psychiatry* (York Beach, ME: Samuel Weiser, 1984), p. 177.

83 According to tradition, because of the influence of demons and astrological factors, choosing to go in certain directions can bring harm.

84 Ngawangthondup Narkyid says that the term "contaminations" refers here to negative external influences that pollute the mind and body. "Pollutions from resentments" [Tib. *khondrib*] refers to instances in which a feeling of ill will arises and remains as a resentment that can eventually lead to illness. Turning the prayer wheel, especially if done with an attitude of compassion toward those you've held bad feelings for, can remove these bad feelings and improve your relations and your health.

85 Manjushri is the manifestation of all Buddha's wisdom. Like Avalokiteshvara, he appears in countless forms as a bodhisattva to inspire and assist others on the path to wisdom.

86 The "five uninterrupted karmas" are the five extremely negative karmic acts that result in rebirth in a hellish state immediately after death—killing one's mother, killing one's father, killing an arhat, wounding a buddha, and causing a schism in the sangha.

87 The "ten nonvirtuous actions" are ten actions, the avoidance of which forms the basis of morality or ethics in Buddhism. These include three bodily actions (killing, stealing, and sexual misconduct), four actions involving speech (lying, harsh speech, slander, and idle gossip), and three mental actions (covetousness, ill will, and holding wrong views.)

88 *Sukhavati,* or the blissful realm, is the pure land of Amitabha. For detailed descriptions of this pure land, see Luis O. Gomez, *The Land of Bliss: The Paradise of the Buddha of Measureless Light* (Honolulu: University of Hawaii Press, 1996).

89 Vajrapani is the manifestation of the power of all the buddhas and is primarily associated with the Vajrayana branch of Mahayana Buddhism.

90 Regarding the five dhyani buddhas, Robert Thurman writes that they are "Archetype Deities representing the five wisdoms: Vairochana, the ultimate reality wisdom; Akshobhya, the mirror wisdom; Ratnasambhava, the equalizing wisdom; Amitabha, the individuating wisdom; and Amoghasiddhi, the all-accomplishing wisdom." See *The Tibetan Book of the Dead* (New York: Bantam Books, 1994), p. 258. In the Buddhist tradition, wisdom is actually the ultimate protection from all inner or outer problems or harms.

91 In Tibetan, *tsangdu.*

92 That is, the life-tree should be aligned so that the top is the natural upper tip of the wood. Other commentaries mention that other materials such as iron can be used for the life-tree or central shaft of the prayer wheel.

93 A page with all of these mantras typed out in the positions in which they should be placed on the life-tree or central shaft of a prayer wheel appears in the third section of this book, which addresses how prayer wheels are actually constructed (see page 92).

94 Diagrams of the sky wheel and earth wheel, prepared by Lama Thubten Zopa Rinpoche, appear in Part Three of this book (see pp 90–91).

95 The *dharmakaya* is one of the three bodies achieved by a buddha. Robert Thurman writes, "At enlightenment the ordinary mind expands in an experience of oneness with the infinity of beings and things, and this becomes a permanent awareness, called the Body of Truth, or Body of Reality. This is the highest fruit of wisdom, a state of virtual omniscience, Nirvana—a perfect, ultimate freedom, and the uttermost fulfillment of all selfish concerns." A buddha also attains or manifests an ethereal *sambogakaya,* or "Body of Beatitude," and a limitless number of *nirmanakaya,* or "Emanation Bodies," which appear in order to work for the infinite benefit of others. See *The Tibetan Book of the Dead* (New York: Bantam Books, 1994), p. 248.

96 The "three kinds of mantra" are gnostic mantra [Tib. *rig-ngag*, Skt. *vidyamantra*], *dharani* mantra [Tib. *zung-ngag*, Skt. *dharanimantra*] and secret mantra [Tib. *sang-ngag*, Skt. *guhyamantra*]. The *Accomplishing the Intent Tantra* (*Gongpa Drubpe Gyu*) says: "'One should know that all mantra are divided into three classes: gnostic mantra, which are the essence of skillful means; dharanis, which are the essence of discriminative awareness; and secret mantra, which are the non-dual pristine cognition.' Thus dharanis are said to originate from the teachings of the Transcendent Perfection of Discriminative Awareness, gnostic mantra from the Kriyatantra and secret mantra from the

Mahayoga, Anuyoga and Atiyoga." See Dudjom Rinpoche, *The Nyingma School of Tibetan Buddhism*, trans. Gurme Dorje & Matthew Kapstein (Boston: Wisdom Publications, 1991), p. 116. The Padmakara Translation Group translates these three as secret mantra, dharani, and awareness mantra. Dilgo Khyentse Rinpoche says, "Of all the many mantras of various kinds, such as awareness mantras, dharanis, and secret mantras, not one is superior to the six syllables of Chenrezi." See Dilgo Khyentse, 1992, p. 58.

97 "Mind-seal deities" [Tib. *yidam*] are personal deities who represent archetypal qualities of the enlightened state of mind. By meditating on them, the practitioner's mind becomes unified with these enlightened qualities, and so the meditator gains realizations. The ones gone to bliss [Skt. *sugatas*] are the buddhas. The "Dharma protectors" are aspects of the buddhas that manifest to remove obstacles for practitioners on their path to enlightenment.

98 A "nearing-the-deity retreat" is also called an "approximation retreat". It is an initial retreat on a mind-seal-deity, during which one usually recites one hundred thousand or more mantras of that deity and one's mind begins approaching the state embodied, or represented, by the deity.

99 That is, with each turning of the prayer wheel, one accumulates the merit or positive energy of having recited the number of mantras that are written inside the wheel. Thus, if a prayer wheel contains one hundred thousand mantras and one turns it ten times, it's as though one had recited a million mantras.

100 Vajrasattva is the manifestation of the purity of all buddhas.

101 The "ten grounds": are levels through which a bodhisattva passes after having directly realized emptiness. Kalu Rinpoche notes that on the first of these grounds, the bodhisattva attains twelve amazing qualities such as "the ability to delve instantaneously into the depths of a hundred different samadhis and to manifest in a hundred different forms to benefit beings." On each subsequent ground one attains "much more profound" realizations and abilities. See *Gently Whispered* (New York: Station Hill Press, 1994), p. 107. The "five paths" refer to five stages that one must go through along the path to enlightenment. A bodhisattva traverses the first two, the paths of accumulation and preparation, by accumulating merit and positive qualities prior to realizing emptiness directly. One realizes emptiness and attains the first ground during the third path, the path of seeing. Then, as one traverses the grounds of a bodhisattva, one also traverses the final two paths, the path of meditation and the path of no more learning. The five bodies and five wisdoms refer to the five dhyani buddhas discussed above.

102 The "eight fetters" presumably refer to the eight conditions in which one does not have the leisure or opportunity to practice Dharma: being born as a hell-

being, hungry ghost, animal, or long-lived god, being born human at a time when no buddha has appeared to teach Dharma, being born in a remote place where no teachings are available, having defective senses (not having the physical or mental capacity to understand the teachings), or upholding wrong views (such as disbelief in the law of karma or in the possibility of enlightenment).

103 It appears that the lineage of the prayer wheel was brought to Tibet during the period of early translations; Lama Zopa Rinpoche says that it was originally brought to Tibet by Padmasambhava himself, and thus the texts quote from him regarding the prayer wheel. Marpa the Translator apparently checked the lineage of the prayer wheel with Naropa, just as he and other translators of his time checked and renewed many aspects of Buddhism in Tibet through their extensive travels and studies.

104 The "Potala pure land" is the pure land of the Buddha of Compassion. As the Dalai Lamas are known as emanations of this buddha, their palace in Lhasa is known as the Potala.

105 According to Lama Zopa Rinpoche, this means that the intended benefits from reading the text are the arising of devotion and the generation of happiness.

106 Throughout the eighteenth and nineteenth centuries, the building of prayer wheels became an important and integral part of the spread of Buddhism to Mongolia. Many of the commentaries cited or translated here were written at the Mongolians' behest. Note the question (below) of the great Mongolian lama, the Fourth Kalka Jetsun Dampa.

107 Jetsun Losang Jampal Gyatso Pal Zangpo was the Eighth Dalai Lama.

108 "The traditional practice of Lama Atisha father and son" presumably refers to the Kadampa tradition founded by Lama Atisha and his Tibetan heart-son, the great master Lama Dromtonpa, who is said to be a previous incarnation of His Holiness the Dalai Lama.

109 Losang Chokyi Gyaltsen was the First Panchen Lama and was renowned as a very great yogi and scholar. His successor, the Second Panchen Lama, was Jetsun Losang Yeshe. That they built many mani wheels and that the Fourth Panchen Lama wrote a commentary on the practice clearly suggests a close connection between the Panchen Lamas and this practice.

110 According to the preface to Sengchen Dorje Chang's collected works, Losang Tenzin Pal Zangpo was one of his personal teachers.

111 *Migtsema* is a praise to Lama Tsongkhapa. Extant in versions of different lengths, it essentially praises Lama Tsongkhapa as embodying the qualities of the Buddha of Compassion, the Buddha of Wisdom, and the Buddha of Power.

112 Apparently, Mingtangpa had a vision of Lama Tsongkhapa, in which he received instructions for making a prayer wheel containing Lama Tsongkhapa's mantra.

113 That is, the practice of the mani wheel was passed down through the early Kagyu lineage in Tibet. The commentary by the Fourth Panchen Lama quotes from the writings of Karma Pagshi, which our current author is also familiar with and highly respects. Karma Pagshi was the second Karmapa and is considered an incarnation of Avalokiteshvara.

114 Although similar to the Fourth Panchen Lama's instructions, the instructions here differ in the placement of mantras on the life-tree, sky wheel, and earth wheel. The instructions in the final section of this book are based on the former.

115 The person rolling the mantras should be clean. They should not have recently eaten meat, garlic, or onions. Their hands should be particularly clean.

116 Presumably each of the eight syllables listed here corresponds to a spoke of the wheel.

117 This mantra contains all the Sanskrit vowels.

118 This mantra contains all the Sanskrit consonants.

119 This is the mantra of dependent arising. It is unclear whether the request above is repeated here.

120 As in the previous commentary, the reference to negative forces from high, low, and intermediate regions suggests negative astrological and planetary forces above; *nagas* below, such as those that are said to cause cancer, leprosy, and the like; and spirits and elemental forces on earth.

121 These are the eight auspicious signs.

122 "Evil-gone realms" here refers to rebirth in the three lower realms—those of hell beings, hungry ghosts, and animals.

123 Apparently the Tibetan name of one of a group of eight bodhisattvas who eliminate obstacles for others.

124 The *Nyung-nay* is a two-day retreat for meditation on the Buddha of Compassion. It involves fasting, doing prostrations, doing visualizations, and reciting mantras and prayers. For a complete explanation of the procedure for engaging in this retreat, see the Seventh Dalai Lama's *Nyung Nä: The Means of Achievement of the Eleven-Faced Great Compassionate One, Avalokiteshvara*, trans. Lama Thubten Zopa Rinpoche & George Churinoff (Boston: Wisdom Publications, 1995).

125 An Indian Buddhist nun, Gelongma Palmo, gained great realizations through the practice of the Compassion Buddha and transmitted the practice of the Nyung-nay meditation retreat. A translation of this *Potoe* prayer appears in the the Seventh Dalai Lama's text.

126 That is, a female who wants to be reborn in a male body will gain this by turning the prayer wheel. Given the cultural contexts of ancient India and Tibet, it is understandable that women wanting the greatest possible access to worldly power or to spiritual teachings and opportunities for solitary retreat might wish for a male form. However, the great Buddhist goddess Tara, who was closely associated with Avalokiteshvara in the Indo-Tibetan tradition, vowed to remain in her female form and attain buddhahood in that way for the benefit of others. Also, the most famous historical meditator on Avalokiteshvara may well be the Indian Buddhist nun, Gelongma Palmo (Skt. *Bikshuni Lakshmi*). So, though accessing spiritual teachings may have been easiest in a male form, the teachings were by no means inaccessible to women.

127 Dr. Cayton and Khamlung Tulku here provide an alternative rendering in English of the Tibetan terms *sang-ngag, zung-ngag,* and *rig-ngag.* As previously noted, these have also been rendered as "secret, gnostic, and dharani mantras" and as "secret, awareness, and dharani mantras."

128 These are the three bodies of a fully enlightened being, a buddha. Thus the prayer wheel as a whole symbolizes the realizations and activities of the three bodies of the buddhas.

129 The poetic rendering of this verse was done with the help of Ngawangthondup Narkyid.

130 This section was translated with the help of Ngawangthondup Narkyid.

131 "Old translations" refers to those done during and just after the first major influx of Buddhism into Tibet (that is, translations of the Nyingma order of Tibetan Buddhism).

132 Dan Martin notes, "The three transitional states [Tib. *bardo*] are: the moment of death, the after-death state, and the time of rebirth."

133 Gungtangpa argues here that the use of external prayer wheels developed from the visualizations in the tantric practices he alludes to, of mantras turning, especially "in the heart center," and points to other external practices that appear to have developed from visualizations.

134 Dan Martin notes that the four actions are classifications for fire rites as well as general motivations prompting ritual activities, namely, peace, growth or increase, influence [control], and force. Without an underlying aspiration for

bringing enlightenment for all beings, these can be ordinary magical, rather than spiritual motives. In this paragraph, Gungtangpa cites a few supporting instances of religious externals that originated from contemplative visualizations.

135 Dan Martin notes, "In a conventional sense, these pellet rites involve physically present pellets distributed as a sacrament, said to grant long life. In the ultimate sense, they relate to the indestructible substance of meditational experience conceived as a drop (or pellet, or seed mantra) in contemplative visualizations. The indestructible drop is said to reside in the heart center."

136 Dan Martin notes that the text by the Fifth Dalai Lama quoted here "does not directly concern prayer wheels, since these dharani rolls are meant to be inserted in (stationary) images or stupas." Nevertheless, Gungtangpa's association of the mantras in the prayer wheel, the dharanis placed in stupas, and the mantras visualized during meditative practices is evocative. His assertion that visualization practices undoubtedly lie "at the origin of the turning of external wheels" appears unsupported by the previous texts.

137 That is, negative karmic imprints on one's consciousness.

138 The "three practices" presumably refers to the three higher trainings—in ethics, meditation, and wisdom—which, combined, lead one to personal liberation from samsara.

Selected Bibliography

Benson, Herbert. *The Relaxation Response.* New York: William Morrow, 1975.

Blofeld, John. *The Tantric Mysticism of Tibet.* Boston: Shambhala Publications, 1987.

Bryant, Barry. *The Wheel of Time Sand Mandala: Visual Scripture of Tibetan Buddhism.* San Francisco: HarperCollins, 1993.

Buswell, Robert E. *The Zen Monastic Experience.* Princeton, NJ: Princeton University Books, 1992.

Campbell, Joseph. *Myths to Live By.* Toronto: Bantam Books, 1972.

Candragomin. *Difficult Beginnings: Three Works on the Bodhisattva Path.* Translated by Mark Tatz. Boston: Shambhala Publications, 1985.

Caswell, James O. *Written and Unwritten: A New History of the Buddhist Caves at Yungang.* Vancouver: University of British Columbia Press, 1988.

Cirlot, Juan E. *A Dictionary of Symbols.* Translated by J. Sage. New York: Barnes & Noble Books, 1971.

Cleary, Thomas (trans.). *The Flower Ornament Scripture: A Translation of the Avatamsaka Sutra, Volume I.* Boston: Shambhala Publications, 1985.

Clifford, Terry. *Tibetan Buddhist Medicine and Psychiatry: The Diamond Healing.* York Beach, ME: Samuel Weiser, 1984.

Conze, Edward (trans.). *The Perfection of Wisdom in Eight Thousand Lines and Its Verse Summary.* San Francisco: Four Seasons Foundation, 1973.

Dagyab Rinpoche. *Buddhist Symbols.* Translated by M. Walshe. Boston: Wisdom Publications, 1995.

Das, Lama Surya. *The Snow Lion's Turquoise Mane: Wisdom Tales From Tibet.* New York: HarperCollins, 1991.

Deshung Rinpoche. *The Three Levels of Spiritual Perception.* Translated by Jared Rhoton. Boston: Wisdom Publications, 1995.

Dogen, Zen Master. *Moon in a Dewdrop*. Edited by K. Tanahashi. San Francisco: North Point Press, 1985.

Dowman, Keith. *Masters of Mahamudra: Songs and Histories of the Eighty-Four Buddhist Siddhas*. Albany, NY: State University of New York Press, 1985.

Drolma, Delog Dawa. *Delog: Journey to the Realms Beyond Death*. Translated by Richard Barron. Junction City, CA: Padma Publishing, 1995.

Dudjom Rinpoche. *The Nyingma School of Tibetan Buddhism: Its Fundamentals and History*. Edited and translated by Gyurme Dorje and Matthew Kapstein. Boston: Wisdom Publications, 1991.

Dumoulin, Herbert. *Zen Buddhism: A History*. Translated by J. W. Heisig and P. Knitter. New York: Macmillan Publishing, 1988.

Eliade, Mircea. *The Sacred and the Profane*. New York: Harvest Books, 1957.

Eppley, K.R., A.L. Abrams, and J. Shear. "Differential Effects of Relaxation Techniques on Trait Anxiety: A Meta-Analysis." *Journal of Clinical Psychology, 45* (1989): 957–74.

Epstein, Mark. *Thoughts Without a Thinker*. New York: Basic Books, 1995.

Getty, Alice. *The Gods of Northern Buddhism*. Translated by J. Deniker. Rutland, VT: Charles E. Tuttle Co., 1962.

Gomez, Louis O. *The Land of Bliss: The Paradise of the Buddha of Measureless Light*. Honolulu: University of Hawaii Press, 1996.

Goodrich, Luther C. "The Revolving Bookcase in China." *Harvard Journal of Asiatic Studies*, VII (1942): 130–65.

Govinda, Lama Anagarika. *Foundations of Tibetan Mysticism*. New York: Samuel Weiser, 1969.

———. *The Psycho-Cosmic Symbolism of the Buddhist Stupa*. Emeryville, CA: Dharma Publishing, 1976.

Gupta, Sagar Mal. *Vishnu and His Incarnations*. Bombay: Somaiya Publications, 1974.

———. *Surya the Sun God*. Bombay: Somaiya Publications, 1977.

Gyal-Tsan, Panchen Lozang Chokyi, The First Panchen Lama. *The Guru Puja*. Translated by A. Berzin, J. Gendun, J. Laine, T. Samten, J. Short, G.N. Dhargyey, and Sharpa Tulku. Dharamsala, India: Library of Tibetan Works and Archives, 1979.

Gyatso, Losang Kalsang, The Seventh Dalai Lama. *Nyung Nä: The Means of Achievement of the Eleven-Faced Great Compassionate One, Avalokiteshvara.* Translated by Thubten Zopa Rinpoche and George Churinoff. Boston: Wisdom Publications, 1995.

Gyatso, Tenzin, The Fourteenth Dalai Lama. *Kindness, Clarity, and Insight.* Edited and translated by Jeffrey Hopkins. Ithaca: Snow Lion Publications, 1984.

————. *Beyond Dogma: Dialogues and Discourses.* Edited by M. Dresser; translated by A. Anderson. Berkeley, CA: North Atlantic Books, 1996.

Hackin, J., Huart, C., Linossier, R., Wilman-Grabowska, H.D., Marchal, C., Maspero, H., Eliseev, S. *Asiatic Mythology.* Translated by F.M. Atkinson. New York: Thomas Y. Crowell Co., 1963.

Hillman, James. *Re-Visioning Psychology.* New York: HarperCollins, 1975.

Hixon, Lex. *Mother of the Buddhas.* Wheaton, IL: Quest Books, 1993.

Holy Bible: King James Version.

Huc, Evariste R. *Travels in Tartary.* Translated by W. Hazlitt. New York: Alfred Knopf, 1927.

Hunter, A. "Tibetan Prayer Wheels." *Arts of Asia,* 15 (1) (1985): 74–81.

Johnson, E.H. *Asvaghosa's Buddhacarita or Acts of the Buddha.* Delhi: Motilal Banarsidass, 1936.

Jung, Carl G. *Symbols of Transformation.* Translated by R.F.C. Hull. Princeton: Princeton University Press, 1956.

————. *Memories, Dreams, Reflections.* Edited by R. Winston and C. Winston; translated by A. Jaffe. New York: Vintage Books, 1961.

————. *Alchemical Studies.* Translated by R.F.C. Hull. Princeton: Princeton University Press, 1967.

Kalu Rinpoche. *Gently Whispered.* New York: Station Hill Press, 1994.

Khyentse Rinpoche, Dilgo. *The Heart Treasure of the Enlightened Ones.* Translated by the Padmakara Translation Group. Boston: Shambhala Publications, 1992.

Kim, Hee-Jin. *Dogen Kigen: Mystical Realist.* Tuscon: University of Arizona Press, 1975.

Ladner, Lorne. "A Mandala Made of Sound." *Mandala: Newsmagazine of the Foundation for the Preservation of the Mahayana Tradition,* (Nov.–Dec. 1995): 42–43.

Martin, Dan. "On the Origin and Significance of the Prayer Wheel According to Two Nineteenth-Century Tibetan Literary Sources." *The Journal of the Tibet Society, 7* (1987):13–29.

Mizuno, Kogen. *Buddhist Sutras: Origin, Development, Transmission.* Tokyo: Kosei Publishing, 1980.

Mullin, Glenn H. *Selected Works of the Dalai Lama I: Bridging the Sutras and Tantras.* Ithaca, NY: Snow Lion Publications, 1981.

———. *Mystical Verses of a Mad Dalai Lama.* Wheaton, IL: Quest Books, 1994.

Nagarjuna. *Nagarjuna's a Drop of Nourishment for People and Its Commentary the Jewel Ornament.* Translated by S. Frye. Dharamsala, India: Library of Tibetan Works and Archives, 1981.

Nagarjuna, and K. Gyatso, The Seventh Dalai Lama. *The Precious Garland and the Song of the Four Mindfulnesses.* Translated by Jeffrey Hopkins, Lati Rinpoche and Anne Klein. New York: Harper & Row, 1975.

Nagarjuna, and Lama Mipham. *Golden Zephyr: Instructions from a Spiritual Friend.* Translated by L. Kawamura. Emeryville, CA: Dharma Publishing, 1975.

Pabongka Rinpoche. *Liberation in the Palm of Your Hand.* Edited by Trijang Rinpoche; translated by Michael Richards. Boston: Wisdom Publications, 1991.

Rabten, Geshe, and Geshe N. Dhargyey, *Advice from a Spiritual Friend.* Boston: Wisdom Publications, 1996.

Rhie, Marilyn, and Robert Thurman. *Wisdom and Compassion: The Sacred Art of Tibet.* New York: Harry N. Abrams Publishers, 1991.

Ribi, Alfred. *Demons of the Inner World.* Boston: Shambhala Publications, 1989.

Roerich, George N. (trans.) *The Blue Annals.* Delhi: Motilal Banarsidass, 1949.

Schopen, Gregory (unpublished manuscript). "A Note on the 'Technology of Prayer' and a Reference to a 'Revolving Book-Case' in an 11th Century Indian Inscription." University of Texas at Austin.

Shabkar, Tsogdruk Rangdrol. *The Life of Shabkar: The Autobiography of a Tibetan Yogi.* Translated by Matthieu Ricard. Albany: State University of New York Press, 1994.

Shantideva. *Siksa-Samuccaya: A Compendium of Buddhist Doctrine.* Translated by C. Bendall and W.H.D. Rouse. Delhi: Motilal Banarsidass, 1922.

Simpson, William. *The Buddhist Praying-Wheel.* New York: University Books, 1970.

Snellgrove, David and Hugh Richardson. *A Cultural History of Tibet*. Boston: Shambhala Publications, 1986.

Strong, John S. *The Legend of King Asoka: A Study and Translation of the Asokavadana*. Princeton: Princeton University Press, 1983.

Suzuki, Daisetz Teitaro. *Manual of Zen Buddhism*. New York: Grove Press, 1960.

Taranatha. *Taranatha's History of Buddhism in India*. Edited by D. Chattopadhyaya; translated by L. Chimpa and A. Chattopadhyaya. Delhi: Motilal Banarsidass, 1970.

Thurman, Robert. *The Central Philosophy of Tibet: A Study and Translation of Jey Tsong Khapa's Essence of True Eloquence*. Princeton: Princeton University Press, 1984.

———. *Essential Tibetan Buddhism*. San Francisco: HarperCollins, 1995.

———. *Inside Tibetan Buddhism: Rituals and Symbols Revealed*. San Francisco: HarperCollins, 1995.

——— (ed.). *Life and Teachings of Tsong Khapa*. Translated by R. Thurman, Sherpa Tulku, Khamlung Tulku, A. Berzin, J. Landaw, and G. Mullin. Dharamsala, India: Library of Tibetan Works and Archives, 1982.

——— (trans.). *The Tibetan Book of the Dead*. New York: Bantam, 1994.

Thurman, Robert and T. Wise. *Circling the Sacred Mountain*. New York: Bantam Books, 1999.

Tsong-ka-pa. *Tantra in Tibet: The Great Exposition of Secret Mantra—Volume 1*. Translated by Jeffrey Hopkins. London: George Allen & Unwin Ltd., 1977.

Tsongkapa and Pabongka Rinpoche. *Preparing for Tantra: The Mountain of Blessings*. Translated by Khen Rinpoche and Michael Roach. Howell, NJ: Mahayana Sutra & Tantra Press, 1995.

Vichta, Kathy. "The Most Beautiful Prayer Wheel in the World." *Mandala: Newsmagazine of the Foundation for the Preservation of the Mahayana Tradition*, (July–August 1995): 26–28.

Warren, Henry C. *Buddhism in Translations*. New York: Athaeneum, 1984.

White, Lynn T. *Medieval Religion and Technology: Collected Essays*. Berkeley, CA: University of California Press, 1978.

Wiesel, Elie. *Sages and Dreamers: Portraits and Legends from the Jewish Tradition*. New York: Simon & Schuster, 1991.

Willis, Janice D. *Enlightened Beings: Life Stories from the Ganden Oral Tradition.* Boston: Wisdom Publications, 1995.

Willson, Martin. *In Praise of Tara: Songs to the Savioress.* Boston: Wisdom Publications, 1987.

Yeshe De Project. *Dharma Wheel Cutting Karma.* Berkeley, CA: Dharma Publishing, 1994.

Yeshe, Lama Thubten. *Introduction to Tantra: A Vision of Totality.* Boston: Wisdom Publications, 1987.

Zopa Rinpoche, Lama Thubten. *The Door to Satisfaction: The Heart Advice of a Tibetan Buddhist Master.* Boston: Wisdom Publications, 1994.

———. "The Power of Prayer Wheels." *Mandala: Newsmagazine of the Foundation for the Preservation of the Mahayana Tradition,* (July–August 1995): 29–30.

Also from Wisdom Publications

WISDOM ENERGY
Basic Buddhist Teachings
Lama Yeshe and Lama Zopa Rinpoche

In this warm and compelling volume, two renowned teachers of Tibetan Buddhism present an entire meditation course. With humor and clarity, Lama Yeshe and Lama Zopa help us to uncover and renounce causes of unhappiness, grasp the purpose of meditation, and realize the advantages of acting with enlightened motives in the interests of all beings.

"A wonderful book, filled with profound wisdom and useful advice. I highly recommend this exceptional book."
—Howard C. Cutler, M.D., co-author of *The Art of Happiness*

0-86171-170-X, 160 pp., paper, $14.95

THE DOOR TO SATISFACTION
The Heart Advice of a Tibetan Buddhist Master
Thubten Zopa Rinpoche

Lama Zopa reveals the essential meaning of an ancient thought-training text that he discovered in his retreat cave high in the Himalayas of Nepal. His message is simple: you can stop all problems forever and gain perfect peace of mind by practicing the thought-training methods explained herein. Open this book and open the door to a timeless path leading to happiness.

0-86171-058-4, 184 pp., paper, $12.50

BUDDHIST SYMBOLS IN TIBETAN CULTURE
An Investigation of the Nine Best-Known Groups of Symbols
Loden Sherab Dagyab Rinpoche

In this fascinating study, Dagyab Rinpoche not only explains the nine best-known groups of Tibetan Buddhist symbols but also shows how they serve as bridges between our inner and outer worlds.

"An excellent summary of symbols used in Tibetan culture. Dagyab Rinpoche goes beyond just presenting a beautiful compendium of symbols and generously tries to convey some of the power and magic that formed the culture of Tibet."
—*Shambhala Sun*

0-86171-047-9, 168 pp., paper, $15.95

THE WORLD OF TIBETAN BUDDHISM
An Overview of Its Philosophy and Practice
His Holiness the Dalai Lama

"The definitive book on Tibetan Buddhism by the world's ultimate authority."
—*The Reader's Review*

"A rare and marvelous opportunity for English-language readers to learn more about [Buddhism and its] spiritual leader." —*Library Journal*

"Written in the Dalai Lama's characteristically straightforward, friendly style which makes these profound teachings accessible to a wide audience." —*Yoga Journal*

"Overall, I cannot think of another work by the Dalai Lama that so thoroughly surveys Tibetan Buddhism. One of the most concise and authentic texts available."—*Religious Studies Review*

0-86171-097-5. 224 pp., paper, $15.95

TIBET GUIDE
Central and Western Tibet
Stephen Batchelor

This completely revised and updated edition of the award-winning *Tibet Guide* is lavishly illustrated with all-new color photographs, maps, monastery floor plans, and rare photos of historic places. Includes phrase book, iconographical guide, and glossary of terms.

"This is the one—a truly important, fascinating, and utterly indispensable guide-book of Tibet." —Richard Gere

0-86171-134-3, 424 pp., paper, $24.95

TIBETAN BUDDHISM FROM THE GROUND UP
A Practical Approach for Modern Life
B. Alan Wallace

"A happy find for anyone seeking to incorporate Buddhist principles into spiritual practice."—*NAPRA ReVIEW*

"One of the most readable, accessible, and comprehensive introductions to Tibetan Buddhism."—*Mandala*

0-86171-075-4, 228 pp., paper, $15.95

HOW TO MEDITATE
A Practical Guide
Kathleen McDonald

What is meditation? Why practice it? How do I do it? The answers to these often-asked questions are contained in this down-to-earth book written by a Western Buddhist nun with solid experience in both the practice and teaching of meditation.

"This book is as beautifully simple and direct as its title." —*Yoga Today*

0-86171-009-6, 224 pp., paper, $14.95

About Wisdom

WISDOM PUBLICATIONS, a not-for-profit publisher, is dedicated to making available authentic Buddhist works for the benefit of all. We publish translations of the sutras and tantras, commentaries and teachings of past and contemporary Buddhist masters, and original works by the world's leading Buddhist scholars. We publish our titles with the appreciation of Buddhism as a living philosophy and with the special commitment to preserve and transmit important works from all the major Buddhist traditions.

If you would like more information or a copy of our mail-order catalog, please contact us at:

Wisdom Publications
199 Elm Street
Somerville, Massachusetts 02144 USA
Telephone: (617) 776-7416 • Fax: (617) 776-7841
Email: sales@wisdompubs.org • www.wisdompubs.org

THE WISDOM TRUST

As a not-for-profit publisher, Wisdom Publications is dedicated to the publication of fine Dharma books for the benefit of all sentient beings and dependent upon the kindness and generosity of sponsors in order to do so. If you would like to make a donation to Wisdom, please do so through our Somerville office. If you would like to sponsor the publication of a book, please write or email us for more information.

Thank you.

Wisdom Publications is a nonprofit, charitable 501(c)(3) organization affiliated with the Foundation for the Preservation of the Mahayana Tradition (FPMT).